How to use *Daily Bread*

Way in

This page introduces both the notes and the writer. It sets the scene and tells you what you need to know to get into each series.

A day's note

The notes for each day include five key elements: Prepare, Read (the Bible passage for the day), Explore, Respond and Bible in a year. These are intended to provide a helpful way of meeting God in his Word.

Prepare yourself to meet with God and pray that the Holy Spirit will help you to understand and respond to what you read.

Read the Bible passage, taking time to absorb and simply enjoy it. A verse or two from the Bible text is usually included on each page, but it's important to read the whole passage.

Explore the meaning of the passage, listening for what God may be saying to you. Before you read the comment, ask yourself: what's the main point of this passage? What is God showing me about himself or about my life? Is there a promise or a command, a warning or example to take special notice of?

Respond to what God has shown you in the passage in worship and pray for yourself and others. Decide how to share your discoveries with others.

Bible in a year If your aim is to know God and his Word more deeply, why not follow this plan to read the whole Bible in one year?

Looking
to heaven

It's been a while since we searched the skies with such a sense of expectation. In 1969 three men journeyed to the Moon in the Apollo 11 command module. Last year's fortieth anniversary celebrations of that historic event have ridden a wave of fresh interest in heavenly exploration. The space race may be gaining a momentum to outstrip the rivalry of the 1960s. The Americans are talking of returning to the Moon, and possibly venturing the 172 million miles to Mars. The Chinese are also planning a Moon landing by 2020. Russia is upgrading its space capability. India and Japan have lunar ambitions too. As for commerce, Sir Richard Branson expects to have paying passengers on 'carbon neutral' spaceships as early as next year.

All this begs huge questions. How is such expense justified when there are so many grave problems on planet Earth? Wouldn't the money be better spent on tackling the environment, poverty or cancer research? The Obama administration estimates the cost of putting man back on the Moon at £114 billion. What couldn't be done with that for the eradication of childhood diseases and the provision of fresh water in the developing world? Some argue that space travel will extend our knowledge boundaries in ways which impact these other challenges.

Christian believers will be found on both sides: some excited by the sheer boundary-breaching adventure of space travel; others campaigning for resources to be spent on humanitarian projects. But as the space race takes off over the next decade, will there be an upsurge of interest in another kind of celestial destination?

The topic of heaven seems, like space travel, to have dropped off the agenda in recent times. Certainly that's true in the western world – a qualification suggesting that the sidelining of our eternal destiny may be related to material prosperity. Heaven was a recurring theme of the

Contents

Never the
same again

This quarter we celebrate both Easter and Pentecost – the most significant events in the history of the world. Just as the first disciples were transformed by them, God wants us too to be changed as we encounter the risen and ascended Lord by the power of his Spirit.

We cannot emphasise enough the significance of the victory Jesus has won over sin, death and hell by his glorious resurrection from the dead. It is 'the launching pad for God's new creation,' as Tom Wright, the bishop of Durham, puts it in a recent article. We look forward to a day soon when there will be no more 'death or mourning or crying or pain' because God will make everything new (Revelation 21:4,5).

But even now, for believers in Jesus, the new creation is experienced: 'the old has gone, the new has come!' (2 Corinthians 5:17). The challenge for each one of us is whether or not we can echo the words of the apostle Paul: 'to me to live is Christ, and to die is gain' (Philippians 1:21).

It's good to welcome Stephanie Heald to the writing team in this issue. Stephanie is an experienced writer and editor, and I'm sure you'll enjoy her comments on Acts as we celebrate the transforming power of the Holy Spirit.

Andrew C. Clark

Editor

songs of the black plantation slaves simply because their conditions were so unbearably awful. The bleakness of daily life forced consideration of the afterlife and a longing for heaven. Are Christians generally so at ease with their lot here on earth that the attractions of heaven are dimmed? Or is there so much confusion surrounding the 'recommended route' to heaven that it's more comfortable to forget it?

Doesn't it seem odd that we pay lip service to the idea of spending eternity in 'a better place, a heavenly homeland' (Hebrews 11:16) but give so little time to preparing for it? We plan for our holidays, our homes, our investments, our retirements... scarcely sparing a thought for the eternal future that will inescapably be ours at a time appointed by God but unknown to us. Some of us look forward to being left money or houses in the wills of older relatives. But Peter tells us of a 'priceless inheritance ... kept in heaven ... pure and undefiled, beyond the reach of change and decay' (1 Peter 1:4).

It hasn't always been so in the history of the Church. Jesus told his followers about the place being prepared in his Father's home. 'When everything is ready, I will come and get you, so that you will always be with me where I am' (John 14:2,3). Paul wrote, '... set your sights on the realities of heaven ... Let heaven fill your thoughts' (Colossians 3:1,2). And for centuries it was a dominant theme. 'I would not give one moment of heaven for all the joys and riches of the world, even if it lasted for thousands and thousands of years,' wrote Martin Luther. Surely the failure of the international banking world that threw the world into financial meltdown and insecurity underlined the folly of relying on money and possessions? 'Don't store up treasures here on earth ... Store your treasures in heaven ... wherever your treasure is, there your heart and thoughts will also be' (Matthew 6:19–21).

Every believer's funeral we attend should be a reminder to us of the imminence and desirability of heaven. When David's baby son was sick, he fasted and wept. But when he died, he refused to mourn. 'Can I bring him back again?' he said. 'I will go to him one day' (2 Samuel 12:23). He was comforted by the certainty of heavenly reunion – as we can be.

CS Lewis said that the reason Christians have become so 'ineffective' in this world is that we have largely ceased to think about the next one.

So we say, 'Amen! Come, Lord Jesus!'

Writer

Lin Ball is a freelance writer and editor, and the chairman of the Association of Christian Writers. She takes on commissions for a number of Christian charities including Scripture Union and Torch Trust for the Blind. She is married to John, a publishing consultant, and they live in Market Harborough. Among her favourite things are walking by the sea, reading novels, playing Scrabble and spending time with her two gorgeous granddaughters, Lily and Mia.

Lifepath Adventure Series

Take a step back in time and discover the life path of key Christian characters, from John Wesley to Mary Jones.

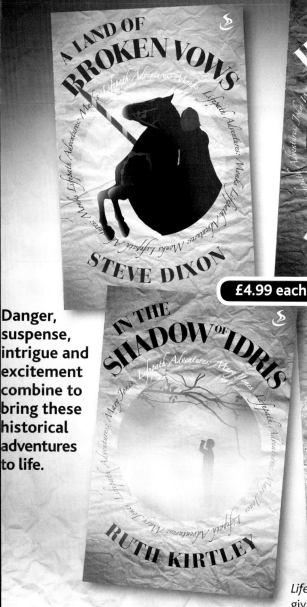

A LAND OF **BROKEN VOWS**
Lifepath Adventures: Monks
STEVE DIXON

HARD ROCK
Lifepath Adventures: John Wesley
FAY SAMPSON

IN THE **SHADOW** OF **IDRIS**
Lifepath Adventures: Mary Jones
RUTH KIRTLEY

PILGRIM
Lifepath Adventures: Pilgrim Fathers
ELEANOR WATKINS

£4.99 each

Danger, suspense, intrigue and excitement combine to bring these historical adventures to life.

Lifepath is a Scripture Union project giving junior school pupils the opportunity to explore their Christian faith through the life path of a well known historic Christian, with a link to the local location. For more details visit
www.scriptureunion.org.uk/lifepath

Failing the test

Prepare

'His works are perfect, and all his ways are just' (Deuteronomy 32:4). Consider before the Lord, your own works and ways.

Read   Mark 15:1–20

Explore

As the spotlight passes over Jesus' friends, the religious and political authorities, the ordinary people (the crowds and the soldiers), we see how each of them has a decision to make. Whether they are Jew or Gentile, each of them fails.

Judas, the disciples and even Peter all fail Jesus their master. The High Priest and Sanhedrin refuse to accept Jesus as their Messiah and, despite his innocence, they plot his death (v 1). Finally the Jewish crowd chooses a murderer over Jesus the life-giver (vs 11–14).

The Gentiles are no better. Pilate, an astute politician (v 10), is trapped by his own attempts to manipulate the Jewish leaders (vs 9–14). He chooses political gain over his duty to uphold justice (v 15).

It could be argued that the Gentile soldiers were simply obeying orders (v 15). However, each soldier is responsible for the part he played in mocking and torturing Jesus (vs 17–20). The motley crew of these verses represents humankind. It doesn't matter whether we claim to know God or not, whether we are leaders or followers. Every time we reject the truth, ignore justice, choose or condone wickedness we are each guilty.

> *Wanting to satisfy the crowd, Pilate released Barabbas to them. He had Jesus flogged, and handed him over to be crucified.*
> Mark 15:15 (NIV)

Respond

'He was crushed for our iniquities ... by his wounds we are healed' (Isaiah 53:5). Spend time quietly considering all Jesus suffered to remove your guilt.

Bible in a Year
Joshua 1–3; Psalm 37

A meaningful death

Prepare

Invite the Holy Spirit to be your guide as you consider the events of that first Good Friday.

Read   Mark 15:21–39

Explore

> *And when the centurion, who stood there in front of Jesus, heard his cry and saw how he died, he said, 'Surely this man was the Son of God!'*
>
> Mark 15:39 (NIV)

Amongst the many people present at this public execution (vs 24,29,31,32,40), only one is said to have searched for meaning in all he saw and heard (v 39). What meaning do you find as you watch the events recorded here?

Here is Jesus, whose awesome power had raised the dead (v 31), willingly submitting to a death the Romans reserved for the worst of criminals, the 'dregs of society'. He is pierced, tormented and reviled by Gentile Rome and the Jewish authorities, and he surrenders to it all without complaint (see Isaiah 53:7). The Jews, like many people today, could not understand it (vs 29–32). Of course, if Jesus had done as they suggested (v 30) he would not be the Messiah whom Scripture had foretold. The job of the Lord's Servant was to save others by suffering and dying in their place (see Isaiah 53:5).

As the darkness of God's wrath and judgement descended (v 33), Jesus faced what we will now never have to face – complete separation from God (v 34). He paid for the sin that separated us from God, a separation represented by the curtain in the temple (v 38). Because of the events of that Friday, we are now free to enter into the holy presence of God.

Respond

Spend time now enjoying what Jesus has won for you – an intimate relationship with God.

Bible in a Year
Joshua 4,5; Romans 10

The cold facts

> Joseph of Arimathea, a prominent member of the Council, who was himself waiting for the kingdom of God, went boldly to Pilate and asked for Jesus' body.
>
> Mark 15:43 (NIV)

Prepare

Come to the Lord with the prayer of Psalm 119:135: 'Make your face shine upon your servant and teach me your decrees.'

Read

Mark 15:40–47

Explore

Jewish society treated women as second class citizens, but Jesus had broken with rabbinic tradition and treated these women as equals with men in the kingdom of God. No wonder they stayed and served him to the bitter end (vs 40,41,47). These women, along with Joseph and the centurion, become crucial witnesses to the fact that Jesus died (vs 44,47). For if Jesus did not really die, then the sin-bearing work on the cross is unfinished and the hope and power of the resurrection is a fantasy.

So Mark leaves no room for theories that Jesus only fainted on the cross, or that bribed soldiers took Jesus off the cross barely alive. Joseph's conversation with Pilate and the ensuing certification of death from an experienced military officer is proof (vs 44,45). The Jewish community might suspect the opinion of Gentiles and women, but the witness of Joseph, a respected member of their ruling Sanhedrin, carried weight. Joseph's every action confirms the cold fact of Jesus' death (v 46). Joseph must have been tormented over his own part in the events that led to Jesus' death (v 43). But as Joseph honoured Jesus publicly, God used him to fulfil Scripture (see Isaiah 53:9) and set the scene for the resurrection.

Respond

Like Joseph, we all fail Jesus. But each new day gives us opportunities to honour him. How will you do that today?

Bible in a Year
Joshua 6,7; Romans 11

 Mark 16:1–20

Clear proof

Prepare

Stand at the threshold of Christ's tomb. It is empty. Offer the Lord your thoughts, your questions, your sense of wonder.

Read

Mark 16:1–20

Explore

Although Jesus had told his followers what would happen, they were all totally unprepared for the events of that Sunday morning. Look at their reactions (vs 8,11,13,14). They need help! So through his messenger (vs 5–7) God provides: *A clear confirmation of events*: 'Yes, this is the tomb of Jesus of Nazareth who died by crucifixion.' *A clear explanation*: 'He is alive, no longer dead.' *A clear proof*: the tomb is empty. *A clear instruction*: 'Go and tell the others.'

And that's all there is to it. But as with all messages from God, the choice is ours – will we believe what God has said? Often our initial response is like that of these early disciples (vs 8,11,13). We dare not believe the unfamiliar, the unprovable.

What does it take to change our minds? An encounter with the risen Lord! For these disciples it was a physical encounter (vs 9,12,14). After his ascension, the Lord meets people in a variety of ways: a voice in Scripture, a message from another believer or in the heart, a picture, a dream, a sense of his presence. We enjoy not just a one-off encounter but a daily experience of his presence as we work with him to bring in his kingdom (v 20).

> *'Don't be alarmed,' he said. 'You are looking for Jesus the Nazarene, who was crucified. He has risen! He is not here. See the place where they laid him.'*
> Mark 16:6 (NIV)

Respond

Be prepared to tell others of your own experience of meeting the Lord, even if you are met with scorn or disbelief.

Bible in a Year
Joshua 8,9; Romans 12

Words
for life

Writer

Mike Hawthorne

Mike has been involved in education all his life but generally reckons he has more to learn these days than before he started. He is now principal of a Christian international school in Dhaka, Bangladesh.

Exodus is a book for modern Christians. This must be so if the God whose guidance we daily seek is the very person who gave these laws to the Israelites thousands of years ago (see Psalm 119:152). The idea that Exodus is primarily of *historical* interest can surely not be right if our God is perfect, unchanging and eternal – how could he then have had different attitudes to what is right and wrong, just because cultures and customs have changed so much over time?

Writing to Timothy, Paul says two things about Scripture: that it is inspired (literally *breathed out*) by God; and that it is profitable (not just of interest) in terms of our practical Christian lives (2 Timothy 3:14–16). This makes an excellent starting point as we consider these ancient writings. By faith we acknowledge God as the source of the ideas and so, whilst we might have many sincere and legitimate questions about them, it is not for us to challenge their authority. Secondly, God's wisdom and judgement being for ever, we can profit a great deal from studying these words in their own right.

But now, before we plunge into some demanding and, at times, very perplexing chapters, I feel personally that I must write the words: *Jesus died for me!* Let's come with Jesus to these passages. Let us thank him that, through his achievement on the cross, God's covenant with Israel has been overtaken by something even more wonderful.

Monday 5 April

Be loved
and obey!

Prepare

Pray that you can share the delight and excitement of the psalmists (see Psalm 19:7–10) about the idea of obeying God's laws.

Read   Exodus 20:1–17

Explore

When was the last time you heard the term 'commandment' used? Few ideas could be less fashionable in this age when we all feel so very much entitled to our own opinions.

But are we? What if the person with the opinion begins by declaring himself as the Almighty God who has just rescued you from slavery? People of Moses' time didn't go in much for democracy and would not have puzzled about inflexible decrees from on high. What is striking about the Ten Commandments in this context is how far they reveal not only God's uncompromising authority (Hammurabi, an earlier king of Babylon whose law code is famous, had plenty of that) but also his loving and devoted nature. The words are radical in several ways.

First, the commandments apply to everyone. Secondly, they are reliable and will not change if, at some future point, it suits those in power to shift the goalposts. Thirdly, the rules are from 'the LORD your God' (v 2) for the people's benefit. A thousand years before Christ's life on earth, we see here God his Father acting in salvation and judgement: it is because God loves his people that he wishes them to obey him.

> 'I am the LORD your God, who rescued you from the land of Egypt, the place of your slavery. You must not have any other god but me.'
> Exodus 20:2,3 (NLT)

Respond

Which of the Ten Commandments do you find most difficult to obey? Ask God to help you with this aspect of life today.

God is here!

'Don't be afraid,' Moses answered them, 'for God has come in this way to test you, and so that your fear of him will keep you from sinning!'
Exodus 20:20 (NLT)

Prepare

In what sense do you believe God is present with you as you approach these verses?

Read

Exodus 20:18–26

Explore

How God chooses to share himself with people is, of course, his business. The revelations of the Lord in this chapter are amazing: first through the commandments and here through this theophany of smoke, thunder, trumpets and so on. Poor Israelites! We might well suspect that 'trembling with fear' (v 18) is something of an understatement…

The images are bound to be mysterious to us. It is fascinating and fun to try to picture the scene but we cannot help but overlay the textual information with our own culturally influenced imaginations. And we must acknowledge that even this revelation is not nearly God in all his fullness. God's people had to wait for the coming of God's Son for that (see John 1:18).

As a part of the book of Exodus, this passage gives us wonderful insights about God and his nature. However, perhaps it is in the context of the Bible as a whole that these words can best be understood. The glimpses offered here of divine glory and wonder are to be developed and confirmed in the final revelation of God's nature in the person and death of the Lord Jesus himself.

Respond

Astonishing, but true – if we want to know what God's really like, we should take a long look at Jesus, and ask to know him better.

Protecting
the vulnerable

Prepare

Spend a short time reflecting on the position of the most oppressed peoples in our modern, global society. Pray for them and then read today's verses.

Read   Exodus 21:1–11

Explore

How are we to reconcile Old Testament edicts with a modern faith? Presumably no *Daily Bread* readers believe that – unlike the Ten Commandments – these specific regulations should be seen as a guidebook prescribing our conduct as Christians today. Part of the answer is that our God is gracious enough to respond to our needs as he finds us – as individuals, as communities and societies in history.

However, linked to this is the uncomfortable truth that our own age is not always so wonderfully enlightened as we like to think. Thousands of years after these rules were written, there are great tracts of the world where no just law holds sway, and where the darkest desires of powerful, anarchic men determine who lives and who dies. In parts of sub-Saharan Africa, children are mutilated for commercial purposes; in remote areas of Asia, women are routinely abused and have no recourse to justice. Even in Western cities, trafficked girls are held captive as prostitutes. Imagine how readily these twenty-first-century citizens would exchange their present plight for the protection of stern desert laws such as the ones outlined here!

> '*If you buy a Hebrew slave, he may serve for no more than six years. Set him free in the seventh year, and he will owe you nothing for his freedom.*'
> Exodus 21:2 (NLT)

Respond

Pray that God will be merciful to the affluent Christians of our modern age who have so ruthlessly disregarded God's expressed wishes, and pray that we will all know how to use God's laws to protect his people.

Make me
a slave?

> But if there is further injury, the punishment must match the injury: a life for a life, an eye for an eye, a tooth for a tooth, a hand for a hand, a foot for a foot …
>
> Exodus 21:23,24 (NLT)

Prepare

How often are our responses dictated to us by non-Christian culture, and how often do we allow the Holy Spirit to show us Jesus' way?

Read
Exodus 21:12–27

Explore

Today's reading seems a particularly harsh set of rules: disobeying the law so often means death. Is this our loving God? Christians' usual response is to set these laws alongside the words of Jesus to demonstrate the way in which his wonderful teaching and his new covenant supersedes the old law. The infamous 'eye for an eye' principle (vs 23–25), for example, is commonly placed in the light of Matthew 5:38–42. Jesus' life, death and resurrection show us a radically different way to make things work.

Although this Jesus-centred response must be right, the danger is that we then allow ourselves casually – even complacently – to skip over the unpalatable aspects of these edicts. What on earth are we to make of verse 21, for example?

In the ancient world, slavery was a reality, much as pollution is one for us. Chapter 21 actually begins with a section instructing masters to show reasonable behaviour towards slaves because the Israelites had been delivered from slavery themselves. The passage also mentions the possibility that a slave might not want to be freed. What if living in the service of a wise, just and loving master is, in truth, the best life available? Are we, in a real sense, meant to be slaves after all?

Respond

Read Matthew 20:26–28, then, if you wish, ask Jesus to make you his slave.

Bible in a Year
Joshua 20–22; Psalm 39

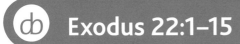
Friday 9 April

Don't ask for justice!

Prepare

Consider the deal you received from life yesterday. Weighing your experience, would you say you got more or less than you deserved?

Read   Exodus 22:1–15

Explore

Two essential aspects of being human are illuminated in this passage. One is the natural instinct that expects justice to be dispensed – a response from someone greater and outside our quarrels, which will restore fairness and order when a wrong has been done. 'It's not fair!' is a cry learned very early in life. These rulings are set out to address issues of justice.

The second aspect is the need for God's presence in the justice process. Our history shows that we humans cannot really do more than botch up the idea of justice. However, if we seek his Spirit, we should sense through these verses the moving of something – some*one* – greater and holier than any human idea. It is clear that God was there first in the making of these laws and then in their outworking.

Notice the status of the judges in verses 9 and 28. These officials eventually combined the roles of magistrate, ruler and holy man. The Israelites were not the only ancient peoples who worked at bringing order to the chaos of human conduct, but it was God's people who truly understood practical justice as an integral part of the religious life of the nation.

> *The neighbour must then take an oath in the presence of the Lord. If the Lord confirms that the neighbour did not steal the property, the owner must accept the verdict, and no payment will be required.*
>
> Exodus 22:11 (NLT)

Respond

Praise our God of justice, and thank him that we will not get what we deserve today!

Will we ever learn?

I will turn your celebrations into times of mourning and your singing into weeping. You will wear funeral clothes and shave your heads to show your sorrow – as if your only son had died. How very bitter that day will be!

Amos 8:10 (NLT)

Prepare

Amos saw Israel as a basket of fruit about to go rotten. What image would you suggest to represent your country? Or your church?

Read   Amos 8:1–14

Explore

A couple of years ago, the economies of the world seemed to be thriving. In the boom times, our 'basket' of commodities was gleaming with luscious fruits – for those with the power and opportunity to grasp them. Now the rottenness which was inherent in our system is apparent to everyone. Consider verse 3 as a representation of the fallen stock markets (the temples!) of these days, and those poor fallen bodies as the millions of newly unemployed. Relevant?

It is clear that our present catastrophe has been caused in large part by greed and neglect of social justice. Amos describes the processes much more graphically and helpfully than the technical explanations we might find for the credit crunch but, essentially, much has continued unchanged through the last 2,700 years.

It is surely right to pray that vulnerable people are spared the worst consequences of our current crisis. What cannot be avoided is the resolve of God, described in verse 7. He is the same God today – he still remembers the corruption of those who should know better. The gross abuse of godly principles and of God's gifts by those in authority in our days will similarly have consequences.

Respond

Let's pray that each of us as individual Christians and the Church as a body might find the words to declare Jesus' response to the economic woes of our time.

Bible in a Year
Judges 1,2; Romans 16

True passion

Prepare

Reflect upon those aspects of life about which you feel truly passionate. Be honest!

Read   Psalm 119:129–152

> *Guide my steps by your word, so I will not be overcome by evil.*
> Psalm 119:133 (NLT)

Explore

Seeking the kinds of 'highs' they see as part of their human rights, people turn to substance abuse, extreme sports and areas beyond the bounds of trusting relationships. Others explore mystic religious experiences or suppose that 'retail therapy' will lead to happiness. The psalmist seems to dwell in the very spiritual places of which so many only dream. Sadly, his state of mind and spirit are probably incomprehensible even to most Christians.

The most remarkable thing about the writer's passion is, perhaps, that his focus is not upon God's gifts, nor his love, or loveliness, nor even on his awesome power and holiness. It is on the *laws* he has laid down: the very stuff we are currently studying. Through these verses, the contrast is between a world in which brutal chaos reigns and one seeking God's purpose. It is in the latter that contentment, joy, even thrills are most likely to be found. Perhaps we find this idea difficult because we have always lived in societies where basic order and security can be taken for granted. Ultimately, these gifts come from the God who sustains the foundations of the world. Living without law and order for a while might make us realise why their restoration should be a cause for ecstatic celebration.

Respond

Why not learn verse 135 by heart?

Monday
12 April

What gets God excited?

> 'You must not mistreat or oppress foreigners in any way. Remember, you yourselves were once foreigners in the land of Egypt.'
> Exodus 22:21 (NLT)

Prepare

Meditate for a couple of minutes on the idea of holiness. Where does this meditation take you?

Read   Exodus 22:16–31

Explore

Further to yesterday's question (what makes you passionate?), in today's reading we are given some insight into the more significant matter of what stirs the feelings of God Almighty. To be sure, he loves holiness and hates sin, reigns on high and delights in his creation. However, it is also striking that, throughout Scripture, we find God not only prescribing codes of social justice but becoming personally engrossed and emotionally committed on behalf of the poor (eg Isaiah 11:4; Amos 5:24).

In verse 22, the people are told not to take advantage of widows and orphans. That's simple enough. But God appears to engage with this issue not as a dispassionate judge weighing the case. Rather, we see him as the unapologetic advocate of the poor, as a powerful friend whose 'anger will be aroused' (v 24) if more privileged citizens try to exploit their weaker compatriots. Studying the instructions about the cloak in verses 26 and 27, we have a vivid illustration of the *compassion* of God, the one who, though ruler of the universe, cares intensely for the poor. The time arrived when God in Christ came down and stood shivering alongside the poor man whose cloak had been stolen.

Response

It is thought that Jesus alludes to this cloak edict in Matthew 5:40. How does he take the idea of social justice even further?

Bible in a Year
Judges 5,6; Psalms 40,41

 Exodus 23:1–19

God in the detail

Prepare

My Bible gives the heading 'Laws of Justice and Mercy' to verses 1–9. Consider the full meanings of these two words by looking in a dictionary.

Read

Exodus 23:1–19

Explore

So powerfully does the energy of Jesus Christ run through these verses that it is as if Exodus 23 and Matthew 5 were written by the same person. And, of course, in one sense they were!

There is no denying that, in many ways, the ancient Israelites were a primitive bunch. They were not amongst the most advanced tribes of their times and they were not the only ones to produce intelligent legal systems. But there is more to these laws than might be found in any ordinary code of practice. Behind the obvious good judgement and order we can sense the compassion of the mind who wrote the words. The instructions almost feel as if Moses, divinely inspired, has gathered around him a small group of followers, into whose eyes he is gazing as he reads out God's words.

Of course, it probably wasn't like that. However, there is a strong connection between these laws, with their close attention to the small details of the rights of the poor, and Jesus' teaching. He cared about the things that concerned the little people, the oxen, donkeys and slaves (v 12). He expected the very best of his disciples (v 19) because he had given everything for them.

'Pay close attention to all my instructions. You must not call on the name of any other gods. Do not even speak their names.'
Exodus 23:13 (NLT)

Respond

Ask yourself how you might best understand and apply verse 19 to your own life.

Bible in a Year
Judges 7,8; Mark 2

God has been there

'You must serve only the
LORD your God. If you
do, I will bless you with
food and water, and I will
protect you from illness.'
Exodus 23:25 (NLT)

Prepare

How do you imagine angels?

Read   Exodus 23:20–33

Explore

While we might be dealing here with a 'classic' angelic being (see, for example, Matthew 28:3), scholars point out that the word 'angel' can also be understood more simply as 'messenger', referring to a divinely appointed human leader such as Moses. But since it says 'my Name is in him' (v 21) it seems more likely we should understand the angel to be a representation of God himself, playing a role similar to the pillars of fire and cloud in Exodus 13:21.

It's wise not to be too dogmatic when peering into events so long back and so far beyond our comprehension. The great news for us is not that we can explain God's way ahead for us. Rather, it is that our God has indeed promised that he will precede us. Wherever he asks us to go, he has been there first and nothing on the path will surprise him. Sensible Christians will not worry too much about how God chooses to support us. The blessed assurance of his involvement in our journeys should be enough.

Before we settle too cosily into this idea, however, it is important to note that God's angel is not merely pottering amiably along. Verse 22 warns us that he will have things to say, and that we'd better pay close attention. God's covenant promise to walk with us is conditional upon us sticking close to him!

Respond

Might we be God's messengers, stepping for him into places where no one else goes with his word?

Thursday
15 April

Approaching God

Prepare

Imagine yourself coming towards Jesus in a place of your choosing. You might, for example, be approaching a building or climbing a mountain.

Read

Exodus 24:1–18

Explore

So much of the story of the Israelites seems to describe elaborate attempts to approach God. Altars are built, beasts are sacrificed and their blood splashed about all through the Pentateuch (the first five books of the Bible). It is clear (eg from Exodus 20:24) that these rituals are carried out at the Lord's command. But really, does it not all seem a long way from God's original purpose: that he might walk with us in the garden in the cool of the day? It is because the Israelites are a messed up people that they need to go through all this palaver before only a few of them can properly meet with their own God.

The Lord keeps himself in a high place. Moses and the elders climb up only after blood and worship are brought together in a way that seems to foreshadow the passion of Jesus himself. In Matthew 26:28, Jesus indeed describes the shared wine as 'my blood of the covenant' (NIV). We are reminded that the Christian's way to an open relationship with God is certainly not an easier route than the one needed by the Israelites. It's just that someone else has done all the slogging up hill, has shed his blood and has become the sacrifice for us.

> *And though these nobles of Israel gazed upon God, he did not destroy them. In fact, they ate a covenant meal, eating and drinking in his presence!*
> Exodus 24:11 (NLT)

Respond

Thank the Lord that we can come to him simply, any time, any place.

Bible in a Year
Judges 11,12; Psalms 42,43

The mercy seat

> I will meet with you there and talk to you from above the atonement cover between the gold cherubim that hover over the Ark of the Covenant. From there I will give you my commands for the people of Israel.
>
> Exodus 25:22 (NLT)

Prepare

What time and place do you find most conducive to worship? Why do you think this is the case?

Read   Exodus 25:1–22

Explore

The instructions for construction of the sanctuary are precise. No scope is left for the human designer and no explanation offered as to why all has to be just so. It is assumed to be enough that God requires total obedience to his master plan. Indeed, could it be that the obedience is actually more important than the numbers of lamps, cherubs and so forth?

In this respect, the God of Israel is as demanding as any of the sundry other gods to be found in the locality. However, these verses reveal features of the one true God that set him apart. First, the people are called to worship not the wonderful golden ark but the one who dwells, invisible above it, at the mercy seat. Then this name for the cover of the ark takes us further into God's true nature. His purpose in setting up the sanctuary is not domination and control. It is so that he might meet with his people and talk to them! And before all that, in verse 1, we see that God himself, rather than demanding the homage which is his right, asks only for the offerings of those who are willing to give.

God is omnipotent – no doubt – but the truth is that he will not force us to worship and love him. His requirements are clear enough. Whether we obey is up to us.

Respond

Seek out a fresh place in which you can worship the Lord.

Saturday
17 April

The all-or-nothing God

Prepare

It is foolish to suppose that we can ever please God by being good, so ask God to show you more today about what it means to know him by faith.

Read   Galatians 3:1–14

Explore

So now we come to it. Here in Galatians is the shocking paradox of God's righteous law. It is a shining light of truth, beauty and joy. And yet, for ordinary people like you, me and the Galatians, it is a wretched, intolerable curse.

This is in large part because God's law is just that: a single covenant. Either we embrace and obey it all, unquestioningly, or else we're doomed. We must conform to every detail: those sections that naturally appeal to us, those we're baffled by and the parts that are frightening. They may scare us either because we know we can't keep these rules, however hard we try, or because we can't understand how our loving Lord could have made such laws in the first place.

But what we think about it is not the point at all. Only by faith can a human being receive anything from God (v 14). It is fascinating that this is also true of the heroes of the Old Testament such as Abraham and Moses (see Hebrews 11:23–31). But our faith does not depend upon anything we can do: only on the good news we have heard about Jesus.

> *Through Christ Jesus, God has blessed the Gentiles with the same blessing he promised to Abraham, so that we who are believers might receive the promised Holy Spirit through faith.*
> Galatians 3:14 (NLT)

Respond

Read 1 John 3:1,2 aloud several times.

Praise God!

You faithfully answer our prayers with awesome deeds, O God our saviour. You are the hope of everyone on earth, even those who sail on distant seas.

Psalm 65:5 (NLT)

Prepare

Aim to empty your mind – just briefly – of all your personal concerns, as you approach this psalm in praise of God. Focus on him.

Read   Psalm 65

Explore

This Sunday reading is exciting because it is about God, not how we feel about him or what we ought to do. Indeed, humanity has only a minor role in the piece. David was evidently inspired to write – and sing – with no purpose other than to praise God himself.

It is a joyful exercise to work through Psalm 65 and list all the reasons why God merits praise. Having, at last, reached the end, we can then return and consider deeper meanings of truths such as 'The river of God has plenty of water ...' (v 9). Little wonder the psalm begins by declaring that 'Praise *awaits* you, God' (v 1, NIV). It is, indeed, almost as if the elements of his creation are forming a polite but eager queue, hoping for their chance to express eternal truths.

At first, these happy verses might seem a long way removed from the severe injunctions of Exodus. Yet here, at the heart of the celebrations, we can find God's order and authority. It is noteworthy that the rest of creation seems very much at ease with this order, accepting the proper place of ridge and furrow without much angst. We humans, alas, need the constant provision of forgiveness in order to join in the party (v 3). But, through Jesus, we can join in at last.

Respond

Take the time to praise God for one of his attributes.

Bible in a Year
Judges 17,18; Mark 6

The path to contentment

Writer

Neil Dougall

Neil lives in North Berwick, a small seaside town in Eastern Scotland, where he is minister of St Andrew Blackadder Church. His wife Helen and two daughters help him keep his feet on the ground.

Western people have never been better off and never been more miserable. In fact since 2008 and the global economic crash, many people's wealth has been hit and they have been left very fearful as well as miserable!

Paul's letter to the Philippians offers a refreshing tonic. It rings with notes of profound joy, sacrificial generosity and deep contentment. The first church Paul planted in Europe was at Philippi (see Acts 16). A deep bond was forged between its members and Paul. They expressed this by sending him money freely and frequently. Remarkably they were the poorest church he'd planted, yet the most generous (see 2 Corinthians 8:1–5).

Paul wrote this letter from his prison cell to do two things. First, to thank them for their latest gift and to commend Epaphroditus who had brought it to him. Epaphroditus had been very ill, and some might conclude he had failed in his mission. Secondly, Paul wrote to encourage the Philippians to live the Jesus way – that is to live out their faith in daily life. He does this by telling them to focus on Jesus and centre their minds on him. He presents Jesus both as example and energy.

My prayer is that reading this letter will help you centre yourself on Jesus, and that as you do this you will discover a profound joy and a deep contentment that has nothing to do with how much or little you have, and that in turn this will prompt you to be generous.

Joyful givers

Prepare

Baked earth, stony ground, dry soil, moist compost: which phrase best describes your heart today? Ask God to soften and moisten the ground as you receive his Word.

Read

Philippians 1:1–11

And I am sure of this, that he who began a good work in you will bring it to completion at the day of Jesus Christ.

Philippians 1:6 (ESV)

Explore

Every teacher said, 'It's a pleasure to have her in the class', reported one of my friends after a parent's evening. I know his daughter; I'm not surprised. Paul's opening words sound a little like this. He thanks God every time he remembers them (v 2), he always prays with joy (v 5), he's confident about their future (v 6), he has them in his heart (v 7), and he prays for more and more (v 9). While not problem-free, the church in Philippi seems to have been healthier and happier than others. Paul's letter peals with notes of joy, generosity and grace. The reason for this is God. It is God 'who began a good work' in them (v 6) – a theme that will recur. But if it's all down to God, why weren't all churches Paul wrote to like this?

In another letter Paul describes the Philippians as poor Christians who gave incredibly generously, as much as, and even more than they could afford (see 2 Corinthians 8:1–5). Could this hold the key? Yes, God was at work, but his Spirit found receptive hearts. The Philippians were joyful, generous, open people who responded eagerly to the Spirit's prompting. That was why Paul could pray with such confidence about their development and growth (v 9).

Respond

God wants to work in your life. Are there attitudes, habits or memories that are making it harder for him to do this?

Bible in a Year
Judges 19,20; Psalm 44

Tuesday 20 April

Generous spirit

Prepare

'You are my beloved child.' Take a moment to enjoy this fact: God loves you for who you are, not for what you've done.

For to me to live is Christ, and to die is gain.
Philippians 1:21 (ESV)

Read

Philippians 1:12–26

Explore

Can you remember a time when your company/ church/community group went forward – but at your expense? If you're like me you felt the personal loss, not the corporate gain. Paul endured this experience but had the opposite reaction to it. He had his freedom taken from him, but could rejoice because this advanced the gospel (v 13). Those who were envious of him preached harder, thinking this might make life tougher for him (v 17). His reaction? 'I don't care, as long as Christ is preached' (v 18). In his shoes I can imagine saying those words, but they wouldn't be true.

Most of the time my vision is defined and confined by my self-interest. I can't seem to escape from my need for praise and approval. Hopefully, at the same time, there is a wider benefit, but if my personal agenda is not met, nothing else seems to count. Paul was not like this. The explanation for his generous spirit seems to have been his experience of Jesus. 'For me to live is Christ, and to die is gain' (v 21). He had developed such a deep relationship with Jesus, the one who models self-giving (see ch 2), that he could reflect that same generosity of spirit.

Respond

Why not make this your prayer today: 'I want to know Christ – yes, to know the power of his resurrection and participation in his sufferings, becoming like him in his death' (3:10, TNIV).

Bible in a Year
Judges 21; Mark 7

29

Gospel reflectors

> Do nothing from rivalry or conceit, but in humility count others more significant than yourselves.
>
> Philippians 2:3 (ESV)

Prepare

Can you see a mirror, some glass or a shiny surface that's reflecting some light? Imagine God's light bouncing off that surface and enlightening you now.

Read   Philippians 1:27 – 2:4

Explore

I am still stunned by the moon. My head knows it has no light of its own. Yet at full moon it's so bright I can ride my bike by its light. I find it hard to believe that its brightness is just a reflection of the sun.

The Philippians had received God's generous grace; now they are expected to reflect that. They are to live a 'manner of life … worthy of the gospel of Christ' (v 27). In practice this means they are to show the love, the mind and the spirit that Christ did (v 2). Sounds simple; it's anything but! While displaying many virtues the Philippian church was anything but perfect. There were disputes and disagreements. Paul has to urge them to strive together (v 27) and to avoid selfish ambition and vain conceit (v 3). Sounds like every church, family or community group I've ever been part of.

Is it possible to break this usual pattern of human interaction? Yes! It's possible, though not easy. While the moon cannot generate light, it can reflect the sun's. We are not asked to generate love for others from within ourselves. Instead as we receive God's grace and love, we can reflect that to others. We receive from God; we give to others.

Respond

Think of a person you're likely to meet that you don't see eye to eye with. Imagine you are a mirror. Ask God to help you reflect his love to them.

Bible in a Year
Ruth 1,2; Mark 8

Thursday 22 April

The gift

Prepare

Any sign of the sun at the moment? Yes? Enjoy it! No? Remember what it feels like to be warmed by its rays.

Read

Philippians 2:5–11

Explore

The sun's energy powers the solar system. Every living thing depends on the light and heat it radiates. For Christians, Jesus has this effect. The self-giving life Paul both models and encourages the Philippians to copy is possible because of Jesus. So Paul says, 'Your attitude should be the same as that of Christ Jesus' (v 5, NIV). His attitude contrasts with what we see around us. Rather than desperately clinging on to what he had, Jesus let go of it (v 6). Instead of fiercely defending himself he allowed others to do their worst to him (v 8). Instead of promoting his own interests he trusted God to do what was right for him (v 9).

A staggering example? Yes. An impossible one to imitate? Yes, if imitation is all Paul's talking about. It's not. Soon he will talk about knowing Christ and being found in him (3:10). Paul is saying that Christ is more than the light that shows the way, he is also the energy that helps us live that way. Christ is held up not just as an example but as an invitation. As we seek Christ, take time to know him and find ourselves more and more in him, he creates within us the desire and capability to live as he lived.

And being found in human form, he humbled himself by becoming obedient to the point of death, even death on a cross.

Philippians 2:8 (ESV)

Respond

'Most merciful Redeemer, Friend and Brother, may we know you more clearly, love you more dearly, and follow you more nearly. Amen' (Richard of Chichester).

A tale of two clichés

Prepare

Picture a swinging pendulum. Ask God to help you find the middle path rather than oscillating between extremes.

Read

Philippians 2:12–18

Explore

God helps those who help themselves! That's what Paul means by 'work out your own salvation' (v 12). *Let go and let God!* Just another way of saying, 'it is God who works in you, both to will and to work for his good pleasure' (v 13). I love the way Paul links these two polarities, seeing no contradiction between them. Living the Jesus way is both something that requires our effort and something we can only do in God's strength.

In and of ourselves we do not have the resources 'to shine as lights in the world' (v 15). We know our own frailties too well. We are filled with good intentions, but struggle to turn them into reality. Yet discipleship is not simply a matter of sitting back and watching God work in us. That's why this passage is full of commands – 'obey' (v 12), 'do all things without grumbling' (v 14), 'hold fast to the word of life' (v 16). Following Jesus is a partnership. He works in us by his Holy Spirit and we cooperate with him by investing effort, energy and will. Remove either of these – our effort or God's strength – and failure is inevitable.

Do all things without grumbling or questioning, that you may be blameless and innocent, children of God without blemish in the midst of a crooked and twisted generation, among whom you shine as lights in the world …

Philippians 2:14,15 (ESV)

Respond

Imagine a yacht gliding along. Its sailor, in one sense, does nothing. The wind moves her boat. In another sense the sailor does everything. Her skill and effort harness the power of the wind. Do you need to stop trying to row your yacht? Do you need to stop sitting and start sailing?

Bible in a Year
1 Samuel 1–3; Mark 9

Saturday
24 April

Why do
I bother?

Prepare

Take a moment to reflect on the sort of week you've had. Tell God how you are feeling and invite him to use this time to help you gain perspective on it.

Read Malachi 3:13–18

Explore

Sooner or later we all experience the sort of disillusionment expressed in verse 14: 'It is vain to serve God.' We make sacrifices for God, serve Jesus faithfully and try hard to live his way. We do not do it for reward but we do expect that life in some way will work better for us. When it doesn't and those who pay no attention to God land on their feet (v 15) we wonder, 'why do I bother?'

God's answer, in effect, is: be patient and don't give up. I haven't forgotten you and will act when the time is right (vs 17,18).

Three assurances are given. If you are trying to live for Jesus, he considers you to be his treasured possession. God's relationship with you is like that of a father and child (not the flawed kind humans often endure, but the ideal). God has not lost his moral compass – he knows the difference between right and wrong and will deal with it justly.

> *Then those who feared the LORD spoke with one another. The LORD paid attention and heard them, and a book of remembrance was written before him of those who feared the LORD and esteemed his name.*
>
> Malachi 3:16 (ESV)

Respond

Think of a possession you treasure. Sometime today get it out, or stand beside it. Touch it, and as you feel it consider how important it is to you and why it means so much to you. Then imagine that you are that treasured possession and that it is God's hand which is touching you. Allow a sense of being special and precious to God to flow through you.

Grumbling or grateful?

Prepare

Do you feel like praising God with all your heart just now (v 1)? Whether the answer is 'yes' or 'no', this psalm can help!

Read   Psalm 138

Explore

A culture of complaint is growing. Nothing is ever quite good enough. We're constantly dissatisfied. What we lack looms much larger than what we have. Worship should counter this. In worship we make a deliberate decision to shift the focus from me and what I lack to God and what he's done. Thanksgiving, the theme of this psalm, is part of worship.

David, the author, makes a deliberate decision to praise God – wholeheartedly (v 1), physically (v 2) and publicly (vs 4,5). He remembers asking God for help, who heard and answered him (v 3). His thanksgiving prompts a sense of wonder. God is exalted, I am lowly, yet he still notices me and helps me (vs 6,7). The result of all this? Confidence for whatever lies ahead (v 8).

It sounds too formulaic to be true – thanks, remembering, reflection, confidence. Did it really happen like this? Perhaps it's been compressed. Yet my experience is that when I push myself to switch from a me-focus to a God-focus, my whole outlook shifts. When I cultivate an attitude of thanks to God, life looks different. I become more content, I discover things about God, and the future seems less fearful.

Respond

Make Psalm 138 your thanksgiving. Make the effort to thank him (vs 1,2). Think of how he's helped you (v 3). Reflect on what this shows you about God (v 6). Place your future in his hands (v 8).

Generous reception

Prepare

Imagine God standing at the door, a huge smile on his face, arms open to welcome you as you choose to spend time with him now.

Read   Philippians 2:19–30

Explore

Sometimes we think it would be better to die gloriously than return in shame. If we set out to do something difficult or dangerous it can be very hard if it all goes pear-shaped and we come back with our tail between our legs. That was Epaphroditus' experience. Hearing that Paul was in prison, the Christians in Philippi sent Epaphroditus with money and instructions to help Paul in any way he could. Epaphroditus, though, became very ill and Paul had to nurse him (v 26). Now, instead of sending this letter with his associate Timothy (v 23), he is sending it with Epaphroditus (v 28). Concerned about the reception he would receive, he lays it on thick: 'Receive him in the Lord with all joy, and honour such men' (v 29).

It's curious how inconsistent people are. The gift the Philippians sent shows how generous they were, but the reception Epaphroditus anticipated shows how mean-spirited they could be. I see it in myself. I'm attracted by the grand gesture; I find the daily act of forgiving and forgetting much harder. I applaud those who make courageous sacrifices; I don't know how to welcome people back when it hasn't worked out.

> *For I have no one like him, who will be genuinely concerned for your welfare.*
> Philippians 2:20 (ESV)

Respond

Do you need to be less condemning and more welcoming of those who have either fallen flat on their faces or made mistakes? What one practical thing might you do in the next day to start?

Bible in a Year
1 Samuel 10,11; Psalms 46,47

Centring prayer

Prepare

'Jesus, be the centre, be my source, be my light, Jesus' (Michael Fyre © 1999 Vineyard Songs/CopyCare).

Read   Philippians 3:1–11

Explore

The Jesus way, spelt out in the last chapter, is immensely attractive but hard to live. How do you 'look not only to [your] own interests, but also to the interests of others' or 'do all things without grumbling or questioning' (2:4,14)? In Philippi, some recommended religious ceremonies (v 3), believing that by pursuing these people would find the life God intended for them. Paul explained that he had tried this. In terms of religious credentials few could compare with him (vs 4–6). Some of this he'd inherited from his family, which he'd then built on with extraordinary zeal and dedication. Yet this way of seeking God, he now believed, had been a complete waste of time. Notice how often he describes his previous way of living as 'loss' (vs 7,8). Far better and more valuable was to know Christ and be found in him (vs 8–10).

Look again at Paul's credentials (vs 4–6). They are all to do with self, achievement and accomplishment. They can't be part of the solution since they are symptoms of the essential problem – our obsession with self. The Jesus way involves changing the perspective so that self no longer sits on the throne, manipulating everything to serve its best interests.

… that I may know him and the power of his resurrection, and may share his sufferings, becoming like him in his death …

Philippians 3:10 (ESV)

Respond

Centring prayer is an ancient practice where a person consciously centres themselves on Jesus. They deliberately shift the focus from themselves and put it on Jesus. Many have found this helps to realign them so that living the Jesus way becomes possible. Why not make verse 10 your centring prayer?

Bible in a Year
1 Samuel 12,13; Mark 12

Wednesday
28 April

Mature
disciples

Prepare

'Rooted and built up in [Christ]' (Colossians 2:7).
Ask God to show you how this might become true
for you.

Read   Philippians 3:12–21

Explore

How do you feel if you overhear someone describe
you as a) immature or b) mature? I guess
a) devastated or b) chuffed! Maturity in discipleship
(v 15) comes as we centre ourselves on Jesus and
work at living his way. Paul mentions three features
of this:

1) *Not arrived* (vs 12–14). Perfectionism is a
constant danger for Christians. As Jesus helps us
to change we can start to think we've made it. To
avoid this danger Paul encourages us to keep looking
ahead to where we're going rather than back at
where we've come from. 2) *Choosing who to copy*
(vs 17,18). No one lives in isolation. Our lives are
shaped by those around us. One sign of maturity
is knowing whose example to follow. God can help
us discern those whose lives reflect the Jesus way.
His Spirit can give us the determination to follow
their example. 3) *Focus* (vs 19–21). Mature disciples
enjoy the good things earth offers but do not
live for them. The phrase 'their god is their belly'
suggests someone who is controlled by food. Other
expressions of this might be their god is their wallet,
car or music. All these are good gifts given for us
to enjoy, but they should not be what we live for.

*I press on toward the
goal for the prize of the
upward call of God in
Christ Jesus.*
Philippians 3:14 (ESV)

Respond

Invite God to highlight
one of these three
things and think of one
thing you might do to
develop in this area.

Thursday
28 April

You are what you think!

'People do not live on bread alone, but on every word that comes from the mouth of God' (Matthew 4:4, TNIV). Prepare to eat God's Word now.

Read   Philippians 4:1–9

Explore

... do not be anxious about anything, but in everything by prayer and supplication with thanksgiving let your requests be made known to God.

Philippians 4:6 (ESV)

The UK TV series *You Are What You Eat* illustrated the connection between what we feed ourselves and our physical well-being. Paul makes a similar connection between what we feed our minds with and our general well-being – you are what you think (v 8).

   Most of us find it difficult to control our minds. Like a butterfly we flit from one thing to another. Without wanting to we find we are thinking greedy, nasty and hateful things. Initially we are shocked: where did that come from? Soon resigned acceptance sinks it – that's just the way I am. Paul disagrees. We are what we think. While we can't filter all the information our minds are bombarded with, we can make deliberate choices about what we focus on. That doesn't mean creating a Christian bubble where only Christian books, music and TV are allowed. It does mean exercising discernment, noticing what ideas and activities are positive, nurturing and wholesome, and choosing to concentrate on them. As we do this we will find it help us to 'stand firm ... in the Lord' (v 1) and live his way (v 5).

Respond

Can you identify a magazine, TV programme, website or podcast you consume which falls foul of Paul's description in verse 8? Might God be prompting you to avoid it?

Bible in a Year
1 Samuel 16,17; Psalm 48

Generosity and contentment

Prepare

Can you think of five good things, big or small, that have happened to you recently? Thank God for them.

Read   Philippians 4:10–23

Explore

And my God will supply every need of yours according to his riches in glory in Christ Jesus.
Philippians 4:19 (ESV)

How much is enough? Enough money, enough holidays, enough chocolate? Most of us discover it's not a fixed amount, it's always a little bit more than what we have. How do we counter this longing to just have a little bit more?

The Philippians countered discontent by developing a generous spirit. From the time they first met Paul they had given freely of the little they had. For some reason they were givers rather than takers (vs 14–19). When we give freely we break the grip of discontent. We prove to ourselves that we don't need more. We discover that the thrill of getting is eclipsed by the joy of giving. Practise generosity and you'll discover it yourself.

Paul countered discontent through centring himself on Jesus (vs 10–13). He's walking a tightrope. He's hugely grateful for the money the Philippians have sent to him with Epaphroditus. But at the same time he hopes they'll understand that his happiness is not dependent on money (v 12). As Paul centred himself on Jesus, striving to know him more and more (3:10), he discovered profound contentment. Able to enjoy material things, he knew that true happiness did not come from them, but through Jesus.

Respond

'Lord, I acknowledge the discontent that lives in me. Change my perspective so I am more contented and generous today. Amen.'

Bible in a Year
1 Samuel 18,19; Mark 14

Saturday
1 May

Optional extras?

> *Therefore, brothers, be all the more diligent to make your calling and election sure, for if you practice these qualities you will never fall.*
>
> 2 Peter 1:10 (ESV)

Prepare

'… you may become partakers of the divine nature' (v 4). 'Lord, I'm not sure what this means, but it's appealing. Show me a little more of how this can happen. Amen.'

Read   2 Peter 1:3–11

Explore

I'm shopping online. I click on the checkout button. The page that appears has all the add-ons I hadn't thought about: insurance, gift wrapping, express delivery? I'm tempted, but I remind myself I don't need them – they're optional extras. Peter encourages us to *add* a whole list of qualities to our faith (vs 5–7). Are things like goodness, godliness and love optional or essential for Christians?

Did you spot the pattern we saw in Philippians 2:12–18? Discipleship is a dance requiring two people. God's power flows through us, and we work at our faith. So Peter says 'His divine power has granted to us all things that pertain to life and godliness' (v 3), but we have to 'make every effort' (v 5). Faith, the bottom rung of Peter's ladder (v 5), is God's gift. We receive it. Then we neither take over nor do nothing. With God's help we climb the ladder, adding one quality at a time. Actually I don't think there is a logical order to the virtues Peter lists. What he's driving at is the idea of progress. Discipleship is a journey. We are called to travel with Jesus, to keep maturing through his power. By this we confirm we really are his people (v 10).

Respond

CS Lewis suggested the way to become loving was by doing loving things. Pick one quality from Peter's list. Think of ways you might actually practise it this weekend.

Bible in a Year
1 Samuel 20–22; Mark 15

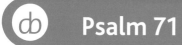
Getting older

Prepare

How do you feel about growing older? Ask God to use this psalm to help you face this inescapable reality.

Read   Psalm 71

Explore

In the West we worship youthfulness. Life expectancy is increasing but we are fearful of old age. Other cultures venerate the elderly, but we are embarrassed by them. This psalm's author was old. In it he expresses his hopes and fears.

Thanks for your support over the years (vs 5–8). Looking back over his life, he recognises God has been with him at every step. He responds by thanking God. Often I only realise how God has helped when I stop and look back.

Don't abandon me when I am old (vs 9). We fear loss of vigour and ability. When I can no longer do things, will people still value me or discard me (vs 11–13)? Is this how God treats us? 'No', according to verse 14. My value to God does not depend on my abilities or performance. He loves me for being me – and that will never change.

Please let me share my wisdom (v 18). Now old and grey, the author longed to share the wisdom he'd discovered with the next generation. A good thing to do, but will they want to hear? For that sharing to happen two things are needed: older people who offer but don't impose wisdom; younger people who are humble enough to accept they might learn.

> *My mouth is filled with your praise, and with your glory all the day.*
> **Psalm 71:8 (ESV)**

Respond

However old you are, read through the psalm again. Stop when you come to a line that resonates with your experience or fear of ageing. Turn it into your prayer.

Bible in a Year
1 Samuel 23,24; Mark 16

Holy to the Lord

Writer

'Tricia Williams

'Tricia is a commissioning editor for SU England and Wales. She is married to Emlyn, and their children Anna and Tom are in the final throes of formal education.

These chapters in Exodus leave us in no doubt about the holiness of God. With the Israelites, you may feel that you need to tread carefully, touch nothing, speak quietly – and keep the rules. Holiness is scary.

Every item, every action, every word, every aspect of life was to be governed by the instructions of God. And when the Israelites rebelled against him, as we'll see, they quickly learnt the awe-fullness of God's holiness. Only when we are filled with his Spirit, only when we give ourselves willingly and whole-heartedly to God's service (as Bezalel and Oholiab did) will we also understand God's everlasting love and faithfulness. And of course, if we didn't have chapters like this in God's Word, we couldn't begin to understand and appreciate the enormity of what God has done for us through the gift of his Son, Jesus.

At the beginning of this series, there is a statement of God's intention for his people: '… that you may know that I, the LORD, sanctify you' (31:13). God began his lessons about holiness in the Sinai desert; the truths of his faithfulness and promises are fulfilled in Jesus – and are still being fulfilled in our lives today. God's people are, like their King, to be different, set apart – holy. Is that the story of our lives?

Let's praise our God in lives that are holy to the Lord – lives which, like Jesus, have different values, attitudes, goals and priorities from those we live among.

Monday 3 May

Holy to the Lord

Prepare

'There are different kinds of gifts, but the same Spirit. There are different kinds of service, but the same Lord' (1 Corinthians 12:4,5, NIV).

Read Exodus 31:1–11

Explore

> *I have filled him with divine spirit, with ability, intelligence, and knowledge in every kind of craft …*
> Exodus 31:3 (NRSV)

What skills, talents and attributes has God given you? What has he called you to do? God had given Moses the plans for the tabernacle (v 11). And he had equipped Moses' team with the necessary gifts to carry them out. Although Bezalel and Oholiab's talents were the artistic, physical skills of craftsmen, they were the result of being filled with God's Spirit (v 3) – and hence no less 'spiritual' than healing or speaking in tongues.

Should it surprise us that God, the divine craftsman, the Creator of the universe, regards such activity as special and holy? Many intricate details are listed here – work in precious stones and metals, working with wood, the making of artefacts for the tabernacle worship, the sewing of the priestly robes.

What plans has God put on our hearts for our churches, our communities, our families, our own lives? It's all too easy to regard some talents as 'ordinary', nothing to do with our holy God. But in these verses we see that it's not just the prophet whose words and work are from the Lord. Everything Bezalel and Oholiab did in God's service was 'Holy to the Lord' (28:36).

Respond

List your own talents and abilities (this is not the time for false modesty!). Why has God given you these? Bring each one to him, asking how he wants you to use this particular gift in his service.

Tuesday
4 May

The Sabbath
principle

Prepare

'The Sabbath was made for man …' (Mark 2:27, NIV).

Read   Exodus 31:12–18

> You yourself are to speak to the Israelites: 'You shall keep my Sabbaths, for this is a sign between me and you throughout your generations, given in order that you may know that I, the LORD, sanctify you.'
>
> Exodus 31:13 (NRSV)

Explore

What do these verses say to us today – to Christians who perhaps work on Saturdays and go shopping on Sundays? The 'Sabbath' was the seventh day of the week, our Saturday. Now it is Sunday – the day of resurrection, the day of the Spirit's coming – that Christians usually set aside as a special day for rest and worship. Jesus himself was criticised for his interpretation of the Sabbath rules and his actions on the Sabbath (Mark 2:24; 3:6; see v 15). So, how do the commandments here fit into our New Testament and twenty-first-century worlds?

There are two things to think about here. First, the point of the Sabbath was to be a sign of the special relationship between God and his people. They were holy, different, set aside (v 13). Second, God's people were to be like him (v 17).

For the Israelites the Sabbath was a blessing from God, not an onerous duty. For us, the Sabbath principle is not intended to be nit-pickingly imposed or self-righteously interpreted (see Colossians 2:16). Saved from having to work for our own salvation, now every day is holy to the Lord. Setting aside specific time to be with God and his people, and for rest, are important, of course. But relationship with God, being different and following him are to be the *constant* markers of our lives.

Respond

How is 'the Sabbath principle' worked out in your life?

Bible in a Year
1 Samuel 27,28; 1 Corinthians 1

No other gods

Prepare

Draw near to Jesus now, who 'always lives to make intercession' for you (Hebrews 7:25).

Read   Exodus 32:1–14

Explore

This is a shocking and sombre tale of God's ancient people. We would never behave like this, would we? Forgetful of God's saving work in their lives, disrespectful to faithful, godly leaders, quick to worship idols, guilty of blasphemy against the Lord's name in their actions, unwilling to stand out from the crowd – no, I'm never like that, am I?

Weak leadership plays a key role. With his brother Moses up on the mountain, Aaron is intimidated by the grumbling, rebellious people. Self-excusing logic might have argued, 'This is the way society today thinks about worship.' After all, bulls (the more likely meaning of 'calf' here) had frequently been connected with idol worship (including in Egypt). Perhaps it could be argued that the golden earrings, probably loot from Egypt, were being offered back to 'God'.

So Aaron goes along with the mob, his words making everything sound OK (v 5). Yet, what is described is a pagan orgy. Aaron and the people are guilty of deliberate idol worship (20:23), sexual excess (20:14) and blasphemy (20:7). Moses, in contrast, intercedes. He is both mindful of God's goodness, holiness, powerfulness – and grace (v 13). In spite of Moses' own anger, he loves his people and pleads for them (see James 5:16).

> *He took the gold from them, formed it in a mould, and cast an image of a calf; and they said, 'These are your gods, O Israel, who brought you up out of the land of Egypt!'*
> Exodus 32:4 (NRSV)

Respond

Pray for your leaders – for wisdom and strength as they exercise tough love in their congregations.

Excuses, excuses

As soon as he came near
the camp and saw the calf
and the dancing, Moses'
anger burned hot, and he
threw the tablets from his
hands and broke them at
the foot of the mountain.

Exodus 32:19 (NRSV)

Prepare

'All that is necessary for the triumph of evil is that good men do nothing' (Edmund Burke).

Read Exodus 32:15–24

Explore

Anything for a quiet life? That's not so easy if you're serious about the Christian faith. After his heavenly mountain-top experience with God, Moses descends to a hell-like vision. 'What on earth did they do to you for you to allow this to happen?', Moses demands of his deputy (v 21). Rightly uncomfortable, Aaron tries some excuses: 'You know what the people are like'; 'It's not easy trying to lead this lot'. He even tried blaming Moses: 'You didn't hurry back, did you?' (vs 22,23). And finally, the sad tale trails off into the realms of fiction: 'I threw the gold into the fire – and out came this calf!' (see 32:4).

The excuses don't wash with Moses: '… you have brought so great a sin upon them' (v 21). Aaron is responsible. Yes, he may have been intimidated and afraid. But his behaviour shows a lack of knowledge of God and a profound absence of trust in God.

In contrast, Moses' response to the situation demonstrates right understanding (v 19) – God alone is holy and worthy of worship. The precious stone tablets crash down the mountain, resonating with the law-breaking activity of God's people. Moses' reaction may seem harsh to us today, but his outrage is right – ultimately we live our lives before a supreme God, not before fickle and sinful men.

Respond

What excuses are leading you and others into sin? Pray for courage to do what is right.

Bible in a Year
2 Samuel 1,2; Psalm 50

Friday
7 May

On the
Lord's side?

Prepare

'Draw near to God, and he will draw near to you'
(James 4:8).

Read   Exodus 32:25 – 33:6

Explore

How does God feel about sin – in our society, in
his Church? In today's western world, the image of
Moses expressing his violent anger and outrage at the
ungodly behaviour of his people is deeply unsettling.
However, it demonstrates that God's holiness and
supremacy is never to be treated lightly. As Christians
we do well to listen to the warning in Paul's words:
'Should we continue in sin in order that grace may
abound?' (Romans 6:1).

Here, the consequence of sin is death. Moses
can only plead, without certainty, for atonement
for the Israelites (v 30). For us, Christ has taken the
punishment – and it's certain that his work is done
(Hebrews 10:12). Still, we also see here glimmers of
hope and God's grace (v 34). And people were given
the opportunity of standing apart for God before the
awful judgement brought by Moses (v 26).

It's not surprising that the Israelites were left
in mourning (v 4). However, their repentance isn't
obvious. It's more that they were troubled by the
absence of God's presence. Yet they do begin to obey
once again – taking off the 'ornaments' which later
would indeed be offered for the worship of God
(ch 35). How often does the sense of God's absence
from our lives warn us that we have strayed from him
– and prompt our return?

> *On the next day Moses
> said to the people, 'You
> have sinned a great sin.
> But now I will go up to the
> LORD; perhaps I can make
> atonement for your sin.'*
> Exodus 32:30 (NRSV)

Respond

'Who is on the Lord's
side?' (Frances R
Havergal). Let's stand
up for him today.

Bible in a Year
2 Samuel 3–5; 1 Corinthians 3

47

God's holy people

Prepare

'Sleeper, awake! Rise from the dead, and Christ will shine on you' (Ephesians 5:14).

Read   Ephesians 5:3–20

Explore

Are we ever guilty of idolatry? Paul describes the person who is guilty of the behaviours he lists (vs 3–5) as 'an idolater'. Idolatry is, in fact, anything which denies God his rightful place in our lives. For the Israelites, their drunken revelry was closely connected with their idolatry and disobedience (ch 32). God's anger with such sin was seen in his consequent judgement. God still judges sin (v 6) – but that judgement has been taken by Christ (v 2). Our thanksgiving for his sacrifice should be seen in our lives – biased unwaveringly to what pleases the Lord (v 10).

So, how should we 'live as children of light' (v 8)? Instead of 'vulgar talk' our lives are to be characterised by thankfulness (v 4). Giving thanks to God 'for everything' (v 20) will constantly keep our minds, words and actions centred on him. We are to 'find out what is pleasing to the Lord' (v 10) and 'understand what the will of the Lord is' (v 17). Decisiveness and deliberate choice are needed. And, if we are filled with the Spirit, then our whole lives will be taken up with pleasing God. Contrary to what those who tempt with 'empty words' might think, living this way brings joy (vs 19,20) – beyond our wildest imaginings.

Respond

Ask the Lord to fill you with his Spirit so you are able to please him today.

Bible in a Year
2 Samuel 6,7; 1 Corinthians 4

Sunday
9 May

What makes you tick?

Prepare

'The LORD, the LORD … abounding in steadfast love and faithfulness' (Exodus 34:6). To God be the glory!

Read   Psalm 115

Explore

'What makes you tick, Mr Williams?' This puzzled question to my (then much younger) husband at a job interview, makes us chuckle now! Emlyn must have communicated different concerns from those of the other interviewees. In today's psalm, we see this contrast – God's people have different values from those who are not his people. Most want a god they can see, hold, confine and control – an idol made in their own image (vs 4–7). Our God is different – and that shows in his people. He is the Maker, the one in control, the one who acts (vs 3,15).

The Israelites stupidly turned from the living God to a useless piece of metal (ch 32). The psalmist points out that if we turn to our idols, it makes our lives just as useless as they are – we're heading for a dead end (v 8). On the other hand, trusting in the one true, living God brings blessing, his help and protection (v 12). The promise is not just for the ancient Israelites, but for everyone who trusts in him (vs 11,13). And he is not a fierce tyrant, but a loving, generous God who gives us families and the whole earth to enjoy (vs 14,16) – gifts that we should use well. The idol worshipper ends up dead (v 17). Those who trust in the Lord will end up praising him 'both now and for evermore' (v 18).

> *Our God is in the heavens; he does whatever he pleases. Their idols are silver and gold, the work of human hands.*
> Psalm 115:3,4 (NRSV)

Respond

Praise the Lord – 'our God' (v 3).

Time with God

Prepare

'… he took them with him and they withdrew by themselves' (Luke 9:10, NIV).

Read   Exodus 33:7–23

Explore

From mountain-top experience to catastrophic outrage – no wonder Moses wants to know where he is with God. Quietness and space seem like a good idea (v 7; see Hebrews 13:13). A tangible sign of meeting with God provides opportunities for unimaginable conversation. Others, drawn by what they see, long again for their God (v 10). Could our unmistakable desire for God also touch others?

So, will Moses and his people stay sitting in the desert? After all, God has told them that he will *not* travel with them (see v 3), although experts suggest that the angel (see v 2) is the embodiment of God's divine presence. Moses, aware of God's holiness and committed to obedience, nevertheless questions his Lord and pleads his case. 'Who's going to help me?' (see v 12). Perhaps Moses is already wondering about the young Joshua (v 11). Whatever, God replies 'I am' (see v 14). Moses reminds God that the Israelites are *his* people (v 13). His presence is what makes them different (v 16). And still, Moses doesn't give up asking for reassurance of God's commitment to him. His bold request (v 18) is not granted exactly, but there's no doubt that Moses has a very close encounter with God. We too often miss seeing God in the moment, but recognise his presence as we look back (v 23).

Respond

'My Presence will go with you, and I will give you rest' (v 14). What is God saying to you?

Bible in a Year
2 Samuel 11,12; Psalm 51

New
start

Prepare

'… we have confidence to enter the Most Holy Place by the blood of Jesus, by a new and living way …' (Hebrews 10:19,20, NIV). Come near to God now.

Read   Exodus 34:1–14

Explore

After failure, after lessons learned, it's time for a new start. God doesn't change. God's *Word* doesn't change (v 1). The giving again of the law follows the pattern of the earlier episode. God's covenant with his people doesn't change either. Here his promises and warnings (vs 10–14) are reiterated. There are two sides to the agreement (v 11). Yes, God will be with his people. Their part is obedience and exclusive faithfulness to him (see Jeremiah 31:32). God is not being cruel or selfish in this. He simply wants to keep his people from harm (v 12). Like a faithful husband, he is jealous for his loved one's good (v 14).

With new awareness of God's holiness and of their sin, his failing people can rejoice again in his goodness: '… a God merciful and gracious, slow to anger, and abounding in steadfast love and faithfulness …' (v 6). And there is a hint in all this of a new covenant to come – which still needs two parties in agreement (see Jeremiah 31:33). But, of course, God's sacredness, the punishment of sin, total forgiveness and relationship with God are summed up and guaranteed in Christ: '… the same yesterday and today and for ever' (Hebrews 13:8).

> *The LORD passed before him, and proclaimed, 'The LORD, the LORD, a God merciful and gracious, slow to anger, and abounding in steadfast love and faithfulness …'*
> Exodus 34:6 (NRSV)

Respond

'… once for all' (Hebrews 10:10, NIV). Praise God for all he has done for you through Jesus.

Glory to God!

> When Aaron and all the Israelites saw Moses, the skin of his face was shining, and they were afraid to come near him.
>
> Exodus 34:30 (NRSV)

Prepare

'Holy, holy, holy is the LORD of hosts…' (Isaiah 6:3). Tread quietly as you come into his presence.

Read
Exodus 34:29–35

Explore

I recently spent some time in a Christian community. There was a sense of holiness and something quite awe-inspiring too, making everyone want to be quiet. It was akin to a right kind of fear, especially when we came together for more formal worship.

Perhaps the descent of Moses from the mountain, radiant from his meeting with God, brought a similar (though, of course, unimaginably greater) sense of untouchable, unbearable holiness (v 29). The Israelites were initially afraid to come near their intermediary. Moses' earlier prayer (33:18) had clearly been answered: he had seen the glory of the Lord – and it had transformed him.

This is a pivotal event woven into the fabric of the whole biblical story. It points us forwards to Jesus himself, the personification of the *new* covenant, glorified on the mountain (see Matthew 17:1,2). Paul, writing to the Corinthian Christians, talks about the meaning of Moses' veil (v 33; see 2 Corinthians 3:7–18). The Israelites couldn't understand the significance of the old covenant because it is 'only in Christ' that the veil is taken away (see Matthew 27:51). Moses was able to enter the tent and, unveiled, talk with God (v 34). This unspeakable privilege is now ours (see 2 Corinthians 3:18, NIV).

Respond

Is the transforming effect of our meeting with God 'unmissable' to others?

Bible in a Year
2 Samuel 15,16; 1 Corinthians 7

More than enough

Prepare

'All things come from you, and of your own have we given you' (1 Chronicles 29:14).

Read   Exodus 35:30 – 36:7

Explore

Do you sometimes feel there isn't enough – money, resources, skills, people – to carry out God's work? Well, here's a story to remember! The Israelites had to be told to stop bringing their gifts, because there was already 'more than enough' (v 7) for the construction of the tabernacle.

We've already met Bezalel and Oholiab. Here now we see the all-encompassing extent of the teamwork. It starts with the words of God and obedience to them (vs 1,5); it's dependent on the Spirit of God giving skills and ability (v 31). Everyone gets stuck in: men, women, craftsmen and artists. Generosity is infectious. It must have been an exciting time.

However, the making of the tabernacle was also dependent on *individual* decisions and *individual* willingness to respond to the Lord's command. I wonder how those whose hearts weren't 'stirred to come' (v 2) and offer what they could, felt once no more was needed. Did they understand that they had excluded themselves from this welcoming of God into their lives? How much do the Lord's word, work and will matter to us? Responding with obedience, hard work and generosity will bring his blessing. Resources for the task? He's given us more than enough!

> *Moses then called Bezalel and Oholiab and every skilful one to whom the LORD had given skill, everyone whose heart was stirred to come to do the work …*
>
> Exodus 36:2 (NRSV)

Respond

What challenging task has God given you or your local church? 'My grace is sufficient for you' (2 Corinthians 12:9).

God
with us

Prepare

'The one who began a good work among you will bring it to completion …' (Philippians 1:6).

Read
Exodus 40:1–16,34–38

Explore

It's nearly two years since the Israelites' miraculous escape from Egypt. They have been through tough times. They have learned of the awfulness of sin, the terror of God's judgement, the awesomeness of his holiness. They've begun to understand that the Lord is compassionate, gracious and forgiving (34:6).

Moses obediently and faithfully sets up the tabernacle. Both this and the priests are consecrated – set apart for service to a holy God. And then, the amazing, unspeakable conclusion to all this: God himself comes to live among them (vs 34,35). It was, as some have suggested, like 'a portable Sinai' (Alec Motyer, *The Message of Exodus*, BST, IVP): God and 'the law' covered with cloud in the midst of the camp.

In spite of the people's past sin and rebellion, the tabernacle becomes the visible symbol of God at the centre of their lives – and he is the one who will direct their onward journey (vs 36,37). So at the end of the Exodus story there is a sense of optimism as the people prepare themselves for the next chapter. God had promised to lead his covenant people to the Promised Land. They could be confident – as we can be – that God would complete the good work he had begun.

Respond

Praise God that, through Jesus, he is with us. Consecrate yourself again to his service as you set out on the next part of your journey with him.

Saturday
15 May

Draw near
to God

Prepare

'Cleanse me from my sin, Lord.'

Read Hebrews 10:19–25

Explore

This is an unbelievable invitation! The Israelites of Moses' day could not have believed it was possible (see Exodus 19:12; 40:35); the ordinary Jews up until the time of Jesus would not have dared imagine it (see Luke 1:9). Whilst God graciously lived amongst his people in the Sinai desert (Exodus 40:34,35), no Israelite would dare come near the holy of holies – not after the lessons of the golden calf. But now, the writer of Hebrews tells us, we can confidently meet with our God (v 19).

The reason? Jesus has ripped aside the curtain (see Luke 23:45) which separates us from our holy Lord. No longer is a symbolic washing bowl for the priests needed (Exodus 40:30–32): we have been made clean by the blood of Jesus.

If that leaves us shaking at the thought of being in God's presence, we are encouraged here to be 'confident'. Just as the Israelites learned that their God is faithful, so we are reminded that 'he who promised is faithful' (v 23). On the other hand, if we've become blasé or over-familiar with our privileged position, perhaps we need to spur one another on, reflecting together again on the cost to Jesus of this 'new and living way' (v 20). Don't give up – but let's encourage each other (v 25).

> *... let us approach with a true heart in full assurance of faith, with our hearts sprinkled clean from an evil conscience and our bodies washed with pure water.*
>
> **Hebrews 10:22 (NRSV)**

Respond

'Lord Jesus, thank you for leading me into the presence of your Father.'

Bible in a Year
2 Samuel 21,22; 1 Corinthians 9

Sunday
16 May

Great is
the Lord!

Prepare

'Every day I will … praise your name' (Psalm 145:2).

Read   Psalm 145

Explore

Is praise relegated to a gated-off, out-of-sight bit of your life? Here, as he often does, David places praise centre-stage (and this was before Jesus!). Apart from the rightness of eternal praise to our God, praise brings life-invigorating blessing for all God's people.

It reminds us of what our God is like: gracious, compassionate, loving, faithful, generous, righteous, holy (vs 8,9,13,16.17,21). It reminds us of what God has done for us: his actions, his gifts, the help he has given (vs 6,12,14,15,16). It reminds us of his faithfulness and his closeness to us (vs 13,18). It encourages and cheers us (v 7). It is a witness to others and future generations of God's good news (vs 4–6,11,12).

Worship was a central part of the Israelites' lives as they recalled all that God had done for them (eg Nehemiah 9:5–15; Psalm 126). It kept them – or brought them back – on track with God. And, with all the down-and-out times of David's life, praise lifted his spirits and renewed his confidence in God for the future (v 20). It is to be part of our daily journeying with God too. Why or how will you exalt God your King today?

Respond

Say this psalm aloud to God – as a prayer of praise. Remember as you do so how God is at work in your life. 'Let every creature praise his holy name' (v 21, NIV).

Bible in a Year
2 Samuel 23,24; 1 Corinthians 10

Sue Wallace

Multi-Sensory WORSHIP

Over 60 ready-to-use prayer activities for creative churches

- Creative, experiential and inspiring
- Ideal for groups or for use in services
- Other *Multi-Sensory* titles available – visit
  www.scriptureunion.org.uk/shop

From the bestselling author of *Multi-Sensory Prayer*

BESTSELLING PHOTOCOPIABLE SERIES

Multi-Sensory Worship is packed full of outlines and scripts to make your times of prayer and praise an opportunity to engage the body and the senses as well as the spirit.

Meet with God using stories, meditation, chanting, painting, recycled objects, crafts, drumming and dance music.

Fully photocopiable with useful indexes by type of prayer, church seasons, Bible verses and group size.

Wind
and fire

Writer

Stephanie Heald

Stephanie is a freelance writer and editor and a member of the 24-7 prayer community. She now lives in the Middle East.

When did you last sense God speaking, in whatever way he might choose to speak?

For many, many years God had been silent. His people were thirsty for him, thirsty for his Spirit, thirsty for him to speak. And then Jesus, full of the Holy Spirit (see Luke 4:1), burst onto the scene, preaching and teaching and healing. Now, in part 2 of that same revival story, God pours out that very same Spirit, just as the prophets had foretold (see Isaiah 44:3; Joel 2:28), just as Jesus had promised. He pours the Spirit out on all people, generously, mercifully, powerfully.

This week we will retell the story of the Church receiving that precious gift, the Holy Spirit, who raised the infant Church to its feet and helped it to take those first few hesitant steps –and who is still helping us to this day!

But some of us may know this story too well, so that it has lost its impact. Over the next week let's take time to sit in the upper room, feel the strong wind from heaven on our faces, see the flicker of tongues of fire, and hear the clamour of God's Word in different voices. Sit with the believers as they start to prayerfully take decisions, mingle with the crowd as Peter preaches God's message, and wonder as the apostles start to do miraculous healings, without the physical presence of Jesus alongside them. And yet, they were not on their own, not at all. And nor are we.

Wait

Prepare

Think of a time when you had to wait: on hold on the phone, or years for an answer to prayer. Note down the feelings that come to mind.

Read   Acts 1:1–11

Explore

So when they met together, they asked him, 'Lord, are you at this time going to restore the kingdom to Israel?'
Acts 1:6 (TNIV)

The apostles had been waiting. For six weeks they had harboured an explosive secret. They were seeing the Lord Christ alive after he'd been clearly and publicly killed. He had been eating and drinking and talking with them, and explaining the kingdom (vs 3,4). But they had also, like most Jews, been waiting for years for the kingdom of Israel to be given back to them. And they had, over three roller-coaster years, seen the lame walk, the sick healed and lives changed. Hope had begun to grow. Now Jesus tells them they only have a few more days to wait.

Expectant, impatient, excited, they ask if it is now that he is going to restore the kingdom (v 6). But they had not understood. They still saw 'kingdom' in worldly, political terms, anticipating independence from Roman rule with Jesus as a priestly King. God's kingdom is far bigger than that. They are also too otherworldly. When Jesus was taken up before their very eyes, he made clear they should not keep waiting for him to keep reappearing. They stand gazing into the sky, looking for something more to happen, for a spiritual resolution. The angels call them back to reality (v 11). Jesus will be back, but now it is time for their work as witnesses to begin.

Respond

Give your waiting time to the Lord, and ask him to use it.

Bible in a Year
1 Kings 1,2; Psalm 55

Trust

Then they prayed, 'Lord, you know everyone's heart. Show us which of these two you have chosen …'

Acts 1:24 (TNIV)

Prepare

Have you had to take a very difficult decision recently? Reflect on how you prayed throughout that time, and the place prayer had in the process.

Read   Acts 1:12–26

Explore

The believers return to Jerusalem and devote themselves to prayer (v 14). This leads to their first decision. You may know what it is like to lose a place of leadership, and the consequent weight of the renewed trust and expectation. Peter must have felt this, and wisely bases his first venture in leading the new community on Scripture (v 20). They all also knew well the significance of the number 12 – the number of the tribes, the number of completeness and the whole people of God. If they were to model the kingdom, they needed to replace Judas.

Appointing an apostle was a solemn matter. The Lord himself prayed all night before choosing the Twelve. The believers had been let down by someone they trusted. Not only had he fallen away, he had betrayed the Lord into the hands of the authorities. Often when we are let down by someone it is difficult to freely trust another in their place. And yet the believers discuss, pray and put it in the hands of God (vs 23–26). The appointment of Matthias is an act of trust which brings a sense of completeness, healing and closure, and allows the community to move on. There is much to be learned from this model of prayerful decision making.

Respond

Think of a time you have let the Lord down. If you need to, ask his forgiveness, and receive his renewed trust.

Bible in a Year
1 Kings 3–5; 1 Corinthians 11

Wind and fire

Prepare

Try to imagine the room that you are in filled with a tornado or struck by lightning. Ask God to give you a glimpse of his power.

Read   Acts 2:1–13

Explore

Jerusalem was filled with visitors – God-fearing Jews from all over the known world gathering (v 5) to give thanks for the first of the harvest, and to celebrate the giving of the law at Sinai. It is here – not in a secret stable or on a lonely mountaintop, but in the middle of a city bursting with people who have come to seek him – that God shows up. The very thing that most of us long to experience in a lifetime actually happens. God, creator of the universe, who has existed from before the beginning of time, is physically present by his Holy Spirit. Wind from heaven fills the whole house. Wind, just like that Elijah felt in the cave. Fire, like Moses saw at the bush that didn't burn up, like the fire that consumed Elijah's soaking sacrifice.

And God speaks. Not through a prophet or priest singled out from others, but through 120 uneducated, uncultured Galileans, so that everyone can hear and understand in their own language (v 8). It is the story of the tower of Babel in reverse. When the visitors eventually go home, they will return changed, taking with them the experience of Pentecost, the Spirit living in them, the law written on their hearts, the first fruits of new life in Christ.

> *Suddenly a sound like the blowing of a violent wind came from heaven and filled the whole house where they were sitting. They saw what seemed to be tongues of fire that separated and came to rest on each of them.*
> Acts 2:2,3 (TNIV)

Respond

Ask the Lord to speak to you in a way that you can understand. Take a moment to listen.

Bible in a Year
1 Kings 6,7; 1 Corinthians 12

Thursday 20 May

Speak out

'God has made this Jesus, whom you crucified, both Lord and Messiah.' When the people heard this, they were cut to the heart and said to Peter and the other apostles, 'Brothers, what shall we do?'

Acts 2:36,37 (TNIV)

Prepare

'Who do you say I am?' (Matthew 16:15). How do you describe Jesus to others? In your own words – try to avoid religious or tired terms – write or speak out who you know him to be.

Read   Acts 2:14–39

Explore

Peter stands up to explain these alarming happenings. The focus of all he says is Jesus – he doesn't dwell on the miracles or take credit for himself and the believers, but points unfalteringly to the risen and ascended Lord. He argues convincingly that the phenomena are from God and foretold in Scripture, quoting the prophet Joel to explain the miracles (vs 17–21), Psalm 16 as foretelling the resurrection (vs 25–28) and Psalm 110 (vs 34,35) to give proof of the Kingship of Christ.

Notice the difference. Once Peter was impulsive, speaking truth from God one moment and discouragement from Satan the next. Now he stands with authority and calms the bewildered crowd, delivers a balanced scriptural interpretation of events, fully ready to 'give a reason for the hope that we have' (see 1 Peter 3:15). Whereas once in fear he had denied the Lord, now in front of thousands he declares Christ as King, not flinching from accusing the Jews of putting him to death. Days earlier he was going fishing. Now he is a true leader, strengthening his brothers, a fisher of men, bringing in a catch greater than on the shores of Galilee. This is the transforming power of the Holy Spirit.

Respond

Pray for the opportunity and power of the Holy Spirit to witness to Christ today.

Bible in a Year
1 Kings 8,9; Psalms 56,57

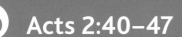
Friday 21 May

New beginnings

Prepare

Who are the five people you care about the most? Think of what they might need or appreciate most today: an email or phone call, an encouraging word, a hand with the dishes, a small gift?

Read

Acts 2:40–47

Explore

Three thousand have heard God's message, have believed and been moved to repentance and baptism. Now what? Like marriage, this is not so much a happy ending as a new beginning, the start of life together. What does this new life look like? There are four foundations. The believers devote themselves to learning from those appointed and discipled by the Lord. They devote themselves to prayer. They break bread, remembering and sharing in Christ's suffering and death on the cross. And they devote themselves to one another (v 42).

The depth of fellowship, marked by the selling of possessions and sharing all things in common (vs 44,45), is deeply challenging. The believers may not all have sold their homes, but that they did sell property had strong implications in that society. Is this how Christians should behave today? This is a holy community, changed from the inside. There is no room for pretending, for half-heartedness. Its authenticity is attested from all sides: from within – they are filled with awe; from above – by wonders and miraculous signs (vs 43); and from without – they enjoy the favour of people (v 47).

> *They devoted themselves to the apostles' teaching and to fellowship, to the breaking of bread and to prayer. Everyone was filled with awe at the many wonders and signs performed by the apostles.*
> Acts 2:42,43 (TNIV)

Respond

Pray for your church community.

Bible in a Year
1 Kings 10,11; 1 Corinthians 13

Restore
and heal

> Take words with you and return to the LORD. Say to him: 'Forgive all our sins and receive us graciously, that we may offer the fruit of our lips.'
>
> Hosea 14:2 (TNIV)

Prepare

Think of someone who has let you down, or a broken relationship. It might be a spouse or parent, a sister or friend. Pray for them.

Read   Hosea 14:1–9

Explore

This chapter concludes Hosea's heartfelt call back to true worship of the Lord. He too has an unfaithful wife, and feels God's deep pain as time after time he forgives Israel, only for her to stray again. Now God calls for a sacrifice of words: words of repentance, words of confession and a promise not to return to idolatry (v 2). He longs to show his love and to heal.

Israel's restoration is described with the imagery of trees. They will be rooted firmly, suggesting constancy and faithfulness rather than waywardness. In dignity they will provide shade and protection like cedars (v 5). Peace and God's provision are evoked by the olive tree, and the land will know abundance and blessing like a blossoming vine (v 7). God himself is a pine (v 8), the source of all fertility, both physical and spiritual. Look also for references that remind you of Jesus: for example, the tree evokes the cross, Jesus' last hours were spent in an olive grove and Jesus called himself the true vine.

Hosea looks forward to a day of repentance and restoration when God's people will know his life, abundance and blessing, as indeed they did because of the cross on the day of Pentecost.

Respond

Write a letter to God about that broken relationship, and read it to him. Allow God space to speak to you – go for a walk or listen to some music.

Bible in a Year
1 Kings 12,13; 1 Corinthians 14

Quench

Prepare

Have you ever lost or left your home? Reflect on how that felt or might feel.

Read

Isaiah 44:1–5

Explore

The people of God are humiliated, homeless and in exile. Now God reminds them how well he knows them, calling them by their old name, Jacob 'the deceiver'. But he also reminds them of all he has done for them, knowing all along what they were like: he formed them, chose them, and called them by name.

He who formed, chose and called them will also help them, now and in the future. He renames them Jeshurun, 'the upright one', and promises to pour out water on the dry ground. For those who are in exile in the desert – where all around is brown and dry, where water is treasured, where streams, trees and meadows are a rare sight – this is a powerful promise.

At Pentecost that day has come. The people knew the humiliation of Roman rule, felt abandoned by God, and were thirsty for him. They longed for him to pour out his Spirit – like water not dripped or splashed but poured out; to hear his voice and know his help and love. Now each hears God's word in their own language, is convicted by and filled with his Spirit, and their thirst is quenched. They begin to live upright lives, like poplar trees by a stream.

For I will pour water on the thirsty land, and streams on the dry ground; I will pour out my Spirit on your offspring, and my blessing on your descendants.

Isaiah 44:3 (TNIV)

Respond

It is tempting to suggest you take a shower or jump in a stream, but pouring a glass of cold water will do. Thank God for his Spirit as you drink it.

Critical yeast

Writer

Andrew Graystone

Andrew is Director of the UK Church and Media Network. He produces and presents programmes for BBC TV and radio. He is often asked to train and advise Christian groups on how best to engage with the fast-changing media environment.

How do you deliver a message to a mass audience in a way that will change them? That's the question that advertisers ask all the time. Usually it's important to generate a 'critical mass' of people who adopt the idea. Traditional media like radio and television are useful because they have the power to reach a lot of people with a simple message. 'This product will change your life,' they tell us. Yeah, right!

But according to Christian peacemaker John Paul Lederach, it's not always necessary to have big numbers to change the world. The vital ingredient for the spread of an idea is not critical mass, but what he calls 'critical yeast'. You may have just a handful of people committed to your message – but if they are the right people in the right places making the right connections, then the idea will multiply rapidly and the result will be unstoppable (see *The Moral Imagination*, OUP, 2005).

That's the effect we see in Luke's account of the explosive growth of the early church. It started with a 'chance' encounter between a lame man and a couple of disciples on their way to the temple. Within weeks there are thousands of new believers – so many that the apostles have to recruit a whole new tier of leaders to serve the community. The active ingredient of course is the Holy Spirit, who really does change lives. Put the Holy Spirit together with a handful of open-hearted worshippers – then stand back and watch how the world changes!

 Acts 3:1–10

Straight in the eye

Prepare

Try to identify just one person you are expecting to meet today who needs to experience God's healing.

Read Acts 3:1–10

Explore

If you are like me, you know what it's like to walk past someone begging in the street, trying not to catch their eye. Peter and John had an appointment to get to. They had no money with them. They had every reason to hurry by. But they didn't. Instead they stopped and looked this man straight in the eye (v 4).

This man had been disabled for all of his forty-plus years (4:22). Like many people today, his life had been so diminished that he had probably given up all hope that it might be different. Peter didn't deal with what he *thought* he needed, but what he *really* needed.

Peter and John had heard Jesus say that they would do 'even greater things' than he had done (John 14:12). Luke wants us to know that the work of believers is to carry on the work of Jesus. We can do that because the 'name' of Jesus has lost none of its power. Jesus had said that his acts of healing were signs of God's kingdom. Now the power of God is in the hands of the disciples: Peter and John, you and me. But if we are going to see Jesus' power at work, we will need to look the world's suffering straight in the eye.

> *But Peter said, 'I don't have any silver or gold, but I do have something else I can give you. By the power of Jesus Christ from Nazareth, stand up and walk!'*
>
> Acts 3:6 (NCV)

Respond

What does it mean for you to look 'straight in the eye' of a needy person today? What might God want to offer them through you?

Broadcast news

Prepare

What's the most surprising thing you've ever seen God do?

Read

Acts 3:11–26

Explore

And suddenly, Peter had an audience! Not surprisingly, news of the remarkable healing spread quickly around the temple courtyards. With the formerly-lame man leaping and dancing around him, Peter grasped the opportunity to explain the significance of what had happened. All of the Old Testament points to Jesus, he told them. And Jesus is responsible for this healing.

It must have been strange for Peter to find himself preaching to a crowd in the very place where Jesus had done the same thing (see John 10:23). Even in the hallowed precincts of the temple, the Galilean fisherman didn't hold back. He told his audience they were ignorant (v 17). He said they were wicked (v 26). He even called them murderers (v 15). It was hardly crowd-pleasing stuff! Perhaps he remembered that Jesus' teaching on that spot had ended with the crowds stoning him. But for all that, his message was charged with good news. Even though you rejected him, Jesus is still at work, still powerful (v 16), still calling for a response (v 19).

Do we sometimes make the mistake of telling our neighbours and our society how far they have fallen, without telling them the good news: 'The promises of God are for you' (see v 25)?

Respond

'Repent … and turn to God … that times of refreshing may come from the Lord' (v 19, NIV).

Bible in a Year
1 Kings 18,19; 1 Corinthians 16

Speak truth to power

Prepare

Who are the powerful people of our age and society? What opportunities do you have to speak to them?

Read Acts 4:1–12

Explore

In the eighteenth century, Quakers defined their mission as 'speaking truth to power'. It's easier said than done. Quite often I find myself speaking to people who are powerful in human terms: politicians, media executives and even religious leaders. I have to stop myself from feeling rather awestruck.

I wonder how Peter and John must have felt as they were questioned by the High Priest's court. Once again they found themselves standing where Jesus had stood. It must have occurred to them that they could suffer the same fate that he had! When Jesus was hauled before the priests he spoke very few words. But Peter and John couldn't help themselves! They couldn't stop speaking about Jesus.

The Sadducees didn't believe in the resurrection of the dead. They wanted to preserve their own power base in the temple, and they wanted no fuss so that their Roman occupiers would let them live in peace. The idea that Jesus was alive and powerful challenged everything they cared about. There's a glorious naivety about Peter's message. He told them that the healing of the lame man was a picture of the salvation offered to everyone through Jesus alone. Either he didn't know what trouble he was getting himself into or else, more likely, he didn't care!

> '*Jesus is the only One who can save people. No one else in the world is able to save us.*'
> Acts 4:12 (NCV)

Respond

'Lord, keep me simple. Make the message of my life as uncompromising and powerful as Peter's. Amen.'

Bible in a Year
1 Kings 20,21; 2 Corinthians 1

69

Unstoppable

> But Peter and John answered them, 'You decide what God would want. Should we obey you or God?'
>
> Acts 4:19 (NCV)

Prepare

Why do you think it's sometimes hard to find the courage to speak openly about Jesus?

Read   Acts 4:13–22

Explore

The age we are living in has a lot in common with the days of the early church. In those days, messages were passed from person to person by word of mouth. Today electronic media like email, mobile phones and the Internet have taken the middle-men out of the communication process. Messages can travel faster than ever before; they can reach more people; and they can't be stopped or controlled. Advertisers use the phrase 'viral marketing' to describe the way products can be powerfully promoted by electronic gossip. Thank God that the electronic media have reopened the floodgates for the Christian message to spread around the world.

This was the dilemma the Jewish leaders faced. They simply couldn't get the lid back on the box! They hoped that they could bully Peter and John into silence, and that somehow the 'viral' spread of the gospel could be contained. No chance! Yesterday Peter and John had seen a lame man walk after 40 years; today everyone in Jerusalem knew about the miracle. Less than a mile away they had Christian friends who had discovered a whole new way of living in generosity and love.

The good news of Jesus is simply unstoppable. Always has been. Always will be.

Respond

Whatever your favourite means of communication, ask the Holy Spirit to give you the same courage that he gave to Peter and John to share the message of Jesus.

Bible in a Year
1 Kings 22; Psalms 60,61

Friday
28 May

Friends reunited

Prepare

Thank God for the community of faith that you belong to.

Read   Acts 4:23–31

Explore

Peter and John may have been bold in front of the Chief Priest, but I'm sure they were relieved to get back to their own people. Just imagine the prayer meeting! They sang Psalm 2 together, with its reminder that God is more powerful than any human ruler. In their worship they reminded each other that God is the Sovereign Lord. The word they used describes a ruler whose power is so great that no other ruler can challenge it.

Worship is about gaining a right perspective on who we are as human beings – with all the dignity that God invests in us – and who God really is too. That kind of worship changes us. Putting God into his rightful place releases us from the struggle to be what we were never meant to be.

If I've completed a difficult or scary job my prayers often amount to: 'Thanks for getting me through that, Lord; now please give me a break!' These disciples prayed: 'Lord, you've seen how tough that was for us. Now give us courage, and do some more!' And after they prayed the place was shaken (v 31) – a strangely reassuring sign from God. As the fourth century theologian John Chrysostom wittily pointed out, 'the place was shaken … but the disciples were not!' (Chrysostom: Homily XI).

After they had prayed, the place where they were meeting was shaken. They were all filled with the Holy Spirit, and they spoke God's word without fear.
Acts 4:31 (NCV)

Respond

Why not use the words of Psalm 2 as a focus for praise, just as the first disciples did?

Bible in a Year
2 Kings 1–3; 2 Corinthians 2

Saturday 29 May

Be the story

> How beautiful is the person who comes over the mountains to bring good news, who announces peace and brings good news, who announces salvation and says to Jerusalem, 'Your God is King.'
>
> Isaiah 52:7 (NCV)

Prepare

If a non-Christian friend met you today, what message would they get from you?

Read   Isaiah 52:7–12

Explore

In the days before radio, troops in battle relied on messengers running from place to place carrying the news. A thousand years before Christ the people of Israel were languishing in captivity. Isaiah pictures them gazing out across the landscape, waiting in hope for a messenger to bring some news. Suddenly, in the distance, they see a man running towards them. And he's smiling. When he arrives, breathless and panting, he can just about get out the good news – 'People of Zion, your enemy is defeated. Your God reigns.'

We too are in a waiting period. We're waiting for God to fulfil his promises of healing, of reconciliation between people and nations, of freedom. So what shall we do in the meantime? Jesus invites us to keep watch; to trust God; to look for signs of freedom arriving.

Those of us who have caught sight of God's future are called to the work of liberation in the mess and the muddle of our present world. Sometimes that means working for justice on the big political stage, and sometimes it's about making changes for good in our own families and neighbourhoods. It's our task to enjoy God today, and to live now in the light of the freedom that is surely coming.

Respond

Wake up, jump up, and get dressed up – because Jesus is coming!

Bible in a Year
2 Kings 4,5; 2 Corinthians 3

Psalm 148

All creation praise

Prepare

Play some music or look at some pictures that help you to appreciate the greatness of God the Creator.

Read   Psalm 148

Explore

On Friday we read about the apostles praising God together. Their praises were just part of a much bigger chorus. This psalm summons the whole of creation to praise God, from top to bottom. See if you can imagine the sound as one layer of praise is heaped upon another.

It starts off way above creation. All the heavenly beings are summoned to praise. Then the sun, moon and stars join in; then the earth, the weather, the animals and plants. Next, kings and princes get the call; then men and women, older people and even children – the lowest of the low in Old Testament times. From top to bottom the whole of creation is called to praise God. Why? Because he's worth it!

Of course we know that heaven is not really 'up there' above the clouds. What this psalm is saying is that there is no dividing line between earth and heaven; between the material and the spiritual world. Every mountain and every molecule vibrates with the praise and the presence of God.

The punch line comes at the end. Can you imagine the whole of earth and heaven praising God? Well, however glorious that sounds, his glory is greater (v 13)!

> *Praise the Lord, because he alone is great. He is more wonderful than heaven and earth.*
> Psalm 148:13 (NCV)

Respond

Allow yourself to be caught up in the praises of creation. Use words if you like, or songs, or the furthest reaches of your imagination.

Letting go

Prepare

'Break me, melt me, mould me, fill me. Spirit of the Living God, fall afresh on me' (Daniel Iverson, © 1965 Birdwing Music/EMI Christian Music Publishing).

Read — Acts 4:32–37

Explore

A few years ago a woman walked into the Building Society where I have my mortgage. She pulled out her savings book containing several thousand pounds, and handed it over the counter. 'I've decided I don't need this,' she said to the astonished assistant. 'Please use it to help some families who are struggling to pay their mortgages.'

What strikes me as remarkable about that woman is not her generosity – though that is pretty astonishing. It is her freedom from the need to control what happened to her own money. It won't surprise you to know that the woman was a Christian. This passage demonstrates that when Christians are filled with the Holy Spirit (v 31) several things happen. Issues that caused disunity and disputes melt away (v 32); tongues which found it hard to speak about Jesus become loosened (v 33); material possessions, money, houses and property lose their grip on their owners (vs 34–37).

This powerful experience emerged from a deep sense of togetherness and dependence on God. It's important to get the order right. We're not filled with the Spirit because we do these things; we do these things because we're filled with the Spirit.

The group of believers were united in their hearts and spirit. All those in the group acted as though their private property belonged to everyone in the group. In fact, they shared everything.
Acts 4:32 (NCV)

Respond

The kind of blessing described in verse 33 only comes to Christians when they are in community. Try to find at least one other Christian today with whom you can pray and share this story.

Bible in a Year
2 Kings 8,9; Psalms 62,63

No compromise

Prepare

I once asked a teenager, 'What is the most difficult thing God could ask you to give up for him?' Her answer was very challenging: 'My image of myself.' How would you have answered?

Read

Acts 5:1–11

Explore

Is it just me, or do you feel a bit of sympathy for Ananias and Sapphira... not to mention their bereaved families? What they did was so *nearly* right. After all they *did* sell their property – or at least some of it. And I'm sure they had the very *best* reasons for holding back part of the money. Perhaps they felt it was responsible to keep something aside for their children. The disciples' experiment in communal living was untested. A few months later they found themselves badly short of cash (11:29). So maybe it was Ananias and Sapphira who were being sensible. Surely they didn't deserve to die?

Some people are called to sell everything they have and give it away. Most are not. But all Christians are called to follow Jesus without limits. What poor Ananias and Sapphira discovered is that trying to be a 50 per cent or even a 99 per cent follower of Jesus is a deadly compromise. That's what Jesus meant by his extraordinary instruction at the heart of the Sermon on the Mount, 'Be perfect, just as your Father in heaven is perfect' (Matthew 5:48). Be wholehearted; single minded; 100 per cent. Anything less is fooling yourself – or lying to God.

> 'Before you sold the land, it belonged to you. And even after you sold it, you could have used the money any way you wanted. Why did you think of doing this? You lied to God, not to us!'
>
> Acts 5:4 (NCV)

Respond

What is God asking you to let go of in order to follow him more closely?

Bible in a Year
2 Kings 10–12; 2 Corinthians 5

Asking
for trouble

Crowds came from all the towns around Jerusalem, bringing their sick and those who were bothered by evil spirits, and all of them were healed.
Acts 5:16 (NCV)

Prepare

Think about your own church or Christian community. How could 'passers-by' find out about it? What might attract them to it? Would it speak to them of God's healing?

Read   Acts 5:12–16

Explore

There's a lot of pressure in our society for faith to be kept in private, between consenting adults. If you practise your faith in public you are asking for trouble. If the apostles felt any similar pressure, they clearly ignored it. The believers met in a very public location. It was the very place where they had got into trouble with the authorities just days before.

There's a lovely contradiction at the heart of this passage. 'None of the others dared to join them …' and yet more and more people were added to their number. We can picture the crowds being irresistibly drawn to the new community, even though they were scared by the power at work in them.

Miraculous signs and wonders are less common today than they were in the first weeks of the Church's life. But as William Barclay puts it, 'The church still exists … that through it miracles of God's grace should happen. People will always throng to a church wherein men's lives are changed' (*The Acts of the Apostles*, St Andrew Press). Faith needs to be practised in public. Church doors should be permanently propped open. If that's asking for trouble, so be it.

Respond

Pray for those Christians who feel pressure to keep their faith to themselves at home or at work. Ask God to give them – and you – wisdom and courage.

Bible in a Year
2 Kings 13,14; 2 Corinthians 6

No
off switch

Prepare

When was the last time you got into trouble for speaking about your faith?

Read   Acts 5:17–42

Explore

The apostles left the meeting full of joy because they were given the honour of suffering disgrace for Jesus.
Acts 5:41 (NCV)

What we call the 'good news' divides people. It makes some people dance for joy. But it makes others very angry. If we are going to witness publicly to our faith in Jesus we had better be prepared to suffer the consequences.

When the powers-that-be felt threatened by the message of the apostles they did what fearful rulers have done throughout the ages – they arrested them. So this time they were *all* in prison. Not that it did much good. You can imprison a person, but you can't contain the Holy Spirit. Wise Gamaliel knew that if God was with these crazy people they would be unstoppable.

For these simple men to find themselves imprisoned, questioned and then flogged must have been profoundly shocking. But they left the Sanhedrin rejoicing. It wasn't that they were happy to be flogged. They were happy that Jesus had chosen them. The seventeenth-century poet Richard Lovelace (1618–1657) is one of many who have been imprisoned for their faith. Yet he wrote: 'If I have freedom in my love and in my soul am free, Angels alone, that soar above, enjoy such liberty' ('To Althea, from Prison').

Respond

Pray for Christians who are in prison – either for their faith or for their crimes. Ask God to enable them to praise him even behind bars.

Friday
4 June

Include
us in

> So, brothers and sisters,
> choose seven of your own
> men who are good, full
> of the Spirit and full of
> wisdom. We will put them
> in charge of this work.
>
> Acts 6:3 (NCV)

Prepare

What sort of people feel marginalised or excluded
from your church congregation? Why?

Read Acts 6:1–7

Explore

On a Sunday morning in my home church about
20 language groups are represented in the
congregation. It's not unusual to have the Bible
reading in Russian, sing a hymn in Spanish, then
have the prayers led in Tamil. One thing that crosses
the language barrier is food – which is why we often
have huge, joyful, multicultural meals together.

For Jewish Christians, the family meal was the
cornerstone of society. And because some people
didn't have immediate family to look after them, the
church developed an early form of social welfare.
Every morning they had a house-to-house collection
for the needy – and every evening there was a
community meal to include those who didn't have a
family to eat with.

One of the key discoveries the apostles made as
the church grew was that there were people who
didn't speak the same language as them but were
still 'full of the Spirit and wisdom' (v 3). After all
they had been through together it was remarkable
that they were so ready to share their leadership.
Remarkable, but vital if the church was to move
forward undivided. Jesus' choice of disciples was
radically inclusive (see Matthew 10:2). We need to
be the same.

Respond

'Lord, give me a
radically inclusive
heart. Help me to
recognise people who
are filled with the
Spirit and wisdom,
even if they aren't like
me. Amen.'

Bible in a Year
2 Kings 17,18; 2 Corinthians 7

Saturday
5 June

The bigger picture

Prepare

'Open my eyes that I may see wonderful things in your law' (Psalm 119:18, NIV).

Read

Nehemiah 7:73b – 8:12

Explore

For nearly two months Nehemiah had been leading the people in the job of rebuilding the walls of Jerusalem. It had been hard physical work, and they had to complete it under armed guard. All through that time they weren't able to gather safely for worship. But now the wall was complete. The first thing they wanted to do was to hear God's Word. They couldn't get enough of it. You can almost hear the crowd cheering for more every time Ezra stopped for breath. 'Go on Ezra ... tell us about the time when...!' So Ezra read the Book of the Law to the people from daybreak till noon. They needed to know how the work they had done fitted into God's bigger picture.

This scene took place 500 years before the events we have been reading about in Acts. In the same temple building where the apostles preached, another crowd gathered to hear the Word of God. Same God. Same story. And as we read together 2,000 years later, we too are part of the same grand narrative.

It's great to study a short passage from the Bible every day. But it's a powerful thing to read the story of God at a stretch. It allows you to appreciate the over-arching purpose of God in history.

> *They read from the Book of the Teachings of God and explained what it meant so the people understood what was being read.*
> **Nehemiah 8:8 (NCV)**

Respond

Try to make time today to reread Acts 3–6 and see how the Holy Spirit worked in the young church.

Bible in a Year
2 Kings 19,20; 2 Corinthians 8

Sunday
6 June

Don't
give up

> The LORD does what is
> right, and he loves justice,
> so honest people will see
> his face.
>
> Psalm 11:7 (NCV)

Prepare

Think back over this week's news. Does it look as if wickedness has the upper hand in the world? Have there been any signs – however small – of God's justice breaking through?

Read   Psalm 11

Explore

The poor man who wrote this psalm was in big trouble. We don't know what the problem was, but he felt the foundations of his life and culture were being destroyed (v 3). Some well-meaning friends have urged him to head for the hills (v 1)! Unusually, this psalm isn't addressed to God. It is his response to those faint-hearted friends.

In a time of great uncertainty, these are the things he knows for sure: *God is still in control.* The twenty-first century is a tough time to be a Christian. But don't imagine that God has lost his grip. He hasn't run away and he hasn't been dethroned (v 4). *God can see what's going on.* God is not distracted or short-sighted. He is watching humanity closely, observing everyone, those who love him and those who don't (v 5). *God will bring about justice in the end.* It's just not in God's nature to let wickedness triumph or leave loose ends untied. If we wait patiently, we will see God face to face. Then we will understand the trials we go through now (vs 6,7).

Respond

If you are feeling discouraged or under pressure, learn this verse and repeat it to yourself through the day: 'Wait for the LORD's help. Be strong and brave, and wait for the LORD's help' (Psalm 27:14).

Bible in a Year
2 Kings 21,22; 2 Corinthians 9

Fresh
bread,
out now!

Don't miss your July–September 2010 issue of *Daily Bread*, available from early August.

Fresh next issue:

Nick Harding
on Revelation

Glenda Trist
on 1 Samuel

Robert Harrison
on Mark

How to order

- through your local Christian bookshop
- by phone 0845 07 06 006 • by fax 01908 856 020
- online www.dailybread.org.uk
- by post Scripture Union (Mail Order) PO Box 5148, Milton Keynes MLO, MK2 2YX
- through your church Bible-reading representative

Or why not subscribe?
See inside the back cover for more details on how to subscribe to *Daily Bread*.

God in
action

Writer

Anna Caroe

Anna is married to Phil and is currently a stay-at-home-mum to 2-year-old Samuel. They're part of the Newfrontiers church in Cambridge and love going to the swings on sunny days.

The book of Judges comes between the books of Joshua and Ruth and covers the time period between the death of Joshua and the rise of the Israelite monarchy.

The people, who have been 'bought' by the Lord and delivered out of Egypt, are receiving their inheritance as they occupy the Promised Land. They are meant to be driving out the Canaanites and getting rid of all their pagan practices. But as the deliverance their ancestors experienced is forgotten, the people begin to turn away from God and instead embrace local pagan culture, morals, rituals and religion.

The events recorded here relate crucially to the extent to which God is honoured and acknowledged as Lord among his people. As they reject and turn further away from him, God allows Israel to experience hardship. When they turn to him again, he delivers them. I find it exciting to see the activity of God in the affairs of his people. It is noticeable how clearly God acts in turning Israel over to their enemies, in raising up a judge, and so delivering his people. Through these events we are also given great perspective on the faithfulness of God towards his precious, though rebellious, people, providing comfort and hope for us too.

The first passage we look at gives a brief overview of the events covered in the book of Judges and places it in historical context. The details of the judges that God raises up are then found in the following chapters.

Visible vs invisible

Prepare

As you prepare to meditate on God's Word, note some of the things occupying your mind. Ask God to help you focus on him now.

Read

Judges 2:6–23

Explore

It's always a good idea to learn from the mistakes of others! Reading about the 'stubborn' ways (v 19) of the people provides us with a great opportunity for our own spiritual health check.

Think about today's popular culture and its 'religions' of fashion, celebrity, sex, sports, possessions and making money. They are popular, attractive and highly visible through magazines, films, TV and the Internet. Their worshippers are vocal and encourage others to join them. Like the Israelites, we too can be guilty of embracing the religions of our highly visible culture at the cost of our relationship with the invisible God.

Of course, I'm not saying that those things in themselves are wrong, or that we should have nothing to do with modern life. In fact, to be effective in sharing our faith we need to be right in the middle of it all, making friendships and genuinely reaching people with God's love. But as the people of God, like Israel in this passage, we're called to be distinct. So we must live immersed in the culture in order to make a difference to it, but always under the Lordship of Jesus so it doesn't overly influence us.

> *When enemies made life miserable for the Israelites, the LORD would feel sorry for them. He would choose a judge and help that judge rescue Israel from its enemies.*
>
> Judges 2:18a (CEV)

Respond

Take the health check! Examine your attitudes to the aspects of culture that affect you most and ask the Holy Spirit to help you come to a godly perspective. There may be things you need to confess to Jesus and there may be practical things you need to change as well.

Bible in a Year
2 Kings 23–25; Psalms 66,67

Faithful feet

Prepare

How do you feel today? Remember that how you feel has no effect on how much God loves you and how much he wants you to spend time with him.

Read   Judges 4:1–24

Explore

Deborah is a strong woman of faith. As a prophetess she leads Israel decisively on the basis of her faith in God. She follows God's plans, judging and making decisions for the people (vs 4–7). Her faith is personal *and* practical. As in the saying 'put your money where your mouth is', her feet were where her faith was!

When she summons Barak, he's not quite so keen to be practical (v 8)! Deborah has told him that God has promised to give him the victory (v 7), but Barak must do the fighting, and when his faith in God is put to this test, it wobbles!

Often we can find ourselves in situations where our personal faith in God has to step up and become practical. For example, when my husband Phil was told his job contract was ending, we had faith that God would provide for us. But that didn't mean that we just sat around waiting for God to drop a job into our laps! Phil had to be faithful 'with his feet' and work on his CV, apply for jobs and go to interviews. As Deborah and Barak put their feet where their faith is, and lead the armies of Israel in battle (vs 14–16), God provides for them (v 23) as he said he would.

> 'I'm not going unless you go!' Barak told her. 'All right, I'll go!' she replied. 'But I'm warning you that the LORD is going to let a woman defeat Sisera, and no one will honour you for winning the battle.'
>
> Judges 4:8,9a (CEV)

Respond

How is your faith visible in your life at the moment? Are there any practical ways in which you need to be 'faithful with your feet' as well as your feelings?

Bible in a Year
1 Chronicles 1–3; 2 Corinthians 10

A visit from God

Prepare

If you knew God was going to call in on you tomorrow, what preparations would you be making? How does that affect how you prepare to read God's Word, worship and pray?

Read

Judges 6:1–24

Explore

Verses 12–16 tell of God's call on Gideon's life. First, God addresses Gideon in a way that is almost entirely opposite to the way that Gideon sees himself (v 15). Secondly, the things God calls Gideon to do, don't seem to fit in with what he's preoccupied with now (vs 3–6) – trying to simply stay alive and provide for his family.

Often we can discount ourselves from God's call on our lives because we don't feel adequate or it doesn't fit in with our plans. Thankfully God knows us better than we know ourselves (see Psalm 139). He calls each of us to relationship with him, to share the gospel with others, to do the works planned for us to do (see Ephesians 2:10) regardless of how we see ourselves or our circumstances. As we follow God's call on our lives, like Gideon (v 16), God promises to be with us (see Matthew 28:19,20) and to bless us (see Romans 8:28).

'Actually, no thanks God, I'm a bit scared and I've got a bit too much on at the minute.' Sound familiar? That could easily have been Gideon's response but, despite their doubts, the people of faith I want to be like don't offer that response to God's calling!

> 'Gideon,' the LORD answered, 'you can rescue Israel because I am going to help you! Defeating the Midianites will be as easy as beating up one man.'
> Judges 6:16 (CEV)

Respond

Have you tried to ignore God on anything recently? What are you going to do about it?

Bible in a Year
1 Chronicles 4–6; 2 Corinthians 11

Go against
the flow

*Gideon chose ten of his
servants to help him,
and they did everything
God had said. But since
Gideon was afraid of
his family and the other
people in town, he did it
all at night.*

Judges 6:27 (CEV)

Prepare

Thank God that he hasn't left us alone, that his
Holy Spirit is with us helping us each day. Ask the
Holy Spirit to help you as you read and pray now.

Read   Judges 6:25–40

Explore

With his very life at stake, Gideon is asked to be
outrageously countercultural and to glorify God
where he has been widely forsaken. I wonder what
he felt when he heard God tell him to destroy his
father's pagan altar (v 25). It was clearly a scary thing
to do because he waited until nightfall
(v 27) and, come the morning, the townspeople
were baying for his blood (v 30). I wonder whether
he knew his father would defend him, or whether he
thought his father would be as angry as the crowd.

Thousands of years later, and our challenge
is remarkably similar. Will we glorify God in
our families, workplaces, neighbourhoods, local
communities, anywhere where we have influence
among our culture? Will we be vocal and practical
about denouncing the false gods our culture raises
up? Will we be genuinely and compassionately
involved in people's lives, enough to help lead them
from worshipping false gods to worshipping the
true God? It's quite a challenge, and not one I feel
particularly prepared for! However, verse 34 says
that 'the Spirit of the LORD came upon Gideon' (NIV).
We rely on the same Spirit of God to empower us in
our battles and to enable spiritual victories.

Respond

The stakes are high.
The Bible is packed
full of people like
Gideon who are asked
to put their lives
on the line for God.
There are countless
more today who risk
their lives simply by
living for Jesus, our
ultimate example of
countercultural
mission. Are you
playing it too safe?

Bible in a Year
1 Chronicles 7–10; Psalm 68

Friday
11 June

A happy ending

Prepare

Thank God for his activity in your life, for how he has worked solutions out for you in the past. Use these things from your past to inspire your worship.

Read   Judges 7:1–25

Explore

Imagine this is a movie. The suspense is really building. The tension between the 'goodies' and the 'baddies' is reaching breaking point. We know the final battle scenes are coming pretty soon. Our main character is rallying the army but secretly feeling a bit worried (see the end of ch 6), having been told to send most of the soldiers home because they're scared! As a cinema audience we can't quite see how the scriptwriters are going to work this out… how can victory possibly be achieved now?

Naturally, the Bible has much better endings than films! As verse 2 explains, God wanted to be crystal clear that only he could work this out and that the victory was his alone. He knew Israel's tendency to forget and be self-reliant, so this was not to be done in their human strength. Thus there was no opportunity for them to boast and God would be glorified once again among them.

God never needs our help. By his grace he chooses to use us in his plans, often to remind us just how great he really is. I've noticed how God steers things in my life to places where only he can bring the solution, so that my life gives more glory to him. It's not easy, but I wouldn't have it any other way!

'Gideon,' the LORD said, 'you still have too many soldiers. Take them down to the spring and I'll test them. I'll tell you which ones can go along with you and which ones must go back home.'
Judges 7:4 (CEV)

Respond

Bring to God things you are struggling with. Ask him to provide solutions and to glorify himself in these situations. Be open to his ways of answering.

Bible in a Year
1 Chronicles 11–14; 2 Corinthians 12

One heart and mouth

And the Scriptures were
written to teach and
encourage us by giving
us hope.
Romans 15:4 (CEV)

Prepare

Thank God that he unconditionally accepts and loves you. His mercy is fresh for you today.

Read

Romans 15:1–13

Explore

It's so easy to be critical of others, isn't it? In today's reading, Paul, speaking to the church in Rome, is clear that there's no place for a critical spirit in the church community. Obviously we shouldn't be judgemental of people who are not Christians, but how much more should we be united as God's people? Paul makes the point (v 6) that as Christians we all worship the same God and it should be in unity, with 'the same heart and mouth'. He is not saying that we all have to agree on everything, but that our inner thoughts and attitudes should honour God by honouring each other, as well as our outward actions and worship.

Jesus accepted us not because of our charm, fashion sense or intelligence, but by grace – in spite of our failings. So we should accept one another in exactly the same way (v 7). Indeed Jesus said that having this sort of love for each other would be the way the rest of the world recognises us as his disciples (see John 13:35).

Paul teaches here that unity is built as we genuinely serve each other, lovingly have patience with each other, bless each other and speak well of each other. Doesn't that sound like a community you'd want to be part of?

Respond

Have you been critical or judgemental of others recently? Have you thought yourself 'better' than someone else for some reason? Are there attitudes you need to repent of or apologies you need to make?

Bible in a Year
1 Chronicles 15,16; 2 Corinthians 13

 Psalm 124

God to the rescue

Prepare

Think of times when God has helped you in difficult circumstances. Use these to inspire your worship.

Read   Psalm 124

Explore

When life is tough it can sometimes feel like God is far away and disinterested in our troubles. However God, by nature, is a rescuer. He loves to break in and rescue his people out of seemingly impossible situations so that he gets the glory as his grace and power are revealed. This is what we saw earlier in the week in Deborah and Gideon's situations.

However, it's something of a never ending story for God's people. The book of Judges is a bit like a see-saw as the Israelites turn to God in their distress then turn away again when life becomes more comfortable. They were quick to forget what God had done for them. Perhaps this is why, many years later, the Jews would sing this psalm to each other as they made their pilgrimage towards Jerusalem each year, to remind themselves of where they would be if it wasn't for God.

We too can point to times in our lives when God has done great things for us and delivered us out of difficult situations, and yet we have even more to be thankful for. As we look to the cross, we can echo the psalm's words as we understand more fully the destiny Jesus has rescued us from and the wonderful future we have been promised instead.

> *Let's praise the LORD!*
> *He protected us from*
> *enemies who were like*
> *wild animals, and we*
> *escaped like birds from a*
> *hunter's torn net.*
> **Psalm 124:6,7 (CEV)**

Respond

It is easy to take these things for granted. Take time now to reflect – where would you be without God?

Bible in a Year
1 Chronicles 17,18; Galations 1

Pilgrim
A Lifepath adventure

"I have been asking God to show me the way forward, whether I should stay here or return with the ship. I have relatives in England who I know would take me in. But – as yet there is no clear answer. I'm still not sure..."

Tom was startled. "Asking God?"

She turned to look at him. "Yes. That is the only sure way of finding guidance for my life."

"But – can you ask him yourself then? I thought – I thought – it was only Elder Brewster and the other leaders who could pray to God..."

Priscilla smiled gently and tucked a stray wisp of hair under her cap. Her tears had dried and she seemed more like her usual cheerful self now. She said, "No, no. Any one of us, man, woman or child, can come to God and ask him freely whatever we will. That is why his Son Jesus died, so that our sins could be washed clean and every one of us have a way into his holy presence. That is why we came here to this place, to be able to come freely before God and worship without ritual devised by man."

"And – does he answer?"

"Oh, yes! Not always in words, but always at the right time, in the right way, when he wills. He knows far better than we know and answers accordingly."

Tom was silent, digesting this information. If anyone could ask God for help, then – did that mean he could too? Even though he was not really one of the Pilgrims? Did God's love reach to him too?

Priscilla looked at him, seemingly able to read his thoughts. She said, "Yes, you too, Tom. You can ask God anything you desire. He loves you and will answer you."

Tom felt a heaviness lift from his heart. God would help him and guide him! He only had to ask. Because God loved him – him, Tom Turner, who belonged to no one.

Maybe he could belong after all, to the settlers and to God. And if he belonged, the hard work, the harsh weather, the disappointments and discouragements could be borne, because he would be sharing them with people who loved and cared.

Priscilla reached out and squeezed his hand, then got to her feet, smoothing down her grey skirts and white apron. "I must get back to my work. Thank you, Tom Turner."

"For what?"

"For happening by. Speaking to you has eased my heart and restored my faith. Now, I think I see what God is saying to me. I think I understand at last what he has been speaking to my heart these past few weeks–"

"And you'll be staying?"

She nodded, her eyes bright again. "I think I will be staying. One or two things need to be settled." She smiled, and her cheeks were suddenly as pink as a wild rose. She said, "And may God guide you too, Tom Turner." And then she was gone, tripping lightly across the sand as though she had not a care in the world.

Tom watched her go, and then turned again to look at the ship, rocking lightly at anchor. He thought he now knew what his own decision would be.

But maybe not his decision alone. He turned his face up to the evening sky and said aloud, "God, I never knew I could ask you to help me. But I'm asking you now, so please let me do what is right. And help me to know you better."

An extract from
***Pilgrim* by**
Eleanor Watkins
978 1 84427 373 7

What is Lifepath?

Lifepath began in 2002, and is an event put on by local Christians for school children aged 7 to 11. It gives pupils the opportunity to explore the life of a Christian or Christians who lived or had influence in the area in which they now live. By studying their story the pupils are able to think about how faith has influenced their actions and to consider what might be the influences in their own lives.

Lifepath is not designed to be a one-off event but a means for the local Christian community to begin or enhance relationships with their local schools. We believe this could be a key tool for groups of churches who want to connect with their local schools, giving them an opportunity to be involved in helping the children of their community to explore the Christian faith.

In many ways Lifepath looks the same wherever it is held and whatever story it is following. The day begins with an opening session for all pupils followed by four workshops and a closing time of worship at about 2pm which allows pupils to return to school for the end of the day. Throughout the day the pupils move around in small groups accompanied by a Lifepath guide.

All pupils should have similar experiences following the four streams of living, believing, exploring and learning. This can be delivered in a number of ways depending on the story studied and the skill of the volunteers involved. From the beginning Lifepath has set out to be both educational and inspirational and is a great opportunity for learning outside the classroom.

Gill Marchant

Gill Marchant, a former teacher, is Scripture Union's Eastern Manager and Schools Consultant. She also manages the Lifepath project.

You be the judge

Have you ever fancied yourself as a judge, with the power to pronounce sentence on people's lives? This week, you'll be doing exactly that. So, to whet your appetite, look at the statements below and decide whether you agree or disagree with each one. Then see if your views change as you read Judges 13–16.

- If people sin, they should be punished.
- Godly parents give you a head start in life.
- The Bible rarely talks about God's anger.
- Leadership is about brains, not brawn.
- God will not honour prayers for revenge.
- When you sin, God deserts you.
- You can't expect a leader to be perfect.

Of course, the book of Judges isn't all about elderly men in gowns and wigs. It's a racy, pacy history, full of fighting, violence, blood and gore that starts eighty years after the first Passover – that fateful night when Moses led the Israelites out of Egypt. And it ends just before Saul is chosen as king. In between (c1195–1050 BC), God raises up 12 leaders to champion Israel's cause. As they move into the Promised Land, their job is to settle disputes within the tribes and to bring God's judgement to the surrounding peoples. Samson is the last and the most colourful of these. Whether he makes you laugh, cry, get angry or feel confused, you cannot ignore this man of power. Why does God pick him to be a deliverer? You be the judge.

Writer

Claire Page

Claire does a mixed bag of teaching, writing and directing whilst cleaning up after three children. She also enjoys being a church warden and belly dancing.

Judges 13:1–23

cd

Wonder struck

Prepare

'Fill me with wonder, Lord, as I come to worship you.'

Read   Judges 13:1–23

Manoah replied, 'Tell us your name, so that we can honour you when your words come true.' The angel asked, 'Why do you want to know my name? It is a name of wonder.'

Judges 13:17,18 (GNB)

Explore

The story of Samson begins like a fairytale: a poor man and his wife, a prediction, and three promises. Remind you of anything? It's funny, too, with the different reactions of Manoah and his wife. But this is not 'Once upon a time'. It is eleventh century BC and no one's laughing. We might be tempted to gloss over the opening lines (13:1) but this information is crucial. If things had not been so bad, God would not have needed judges like Samson. So, what was the evil that the Israelites had done? Read the background in Judges 2:10 – 3:6 to find out.

Despite Israel's sin, there is hope. God can still find people who are in awe of him. Manoah's fear of God (v 22) may seem naive to us, but as Dale Ralph Davis says: 'We must wipe those patronizing smiles off our faces. Christians sometimes have a tendency to read passages like this with their condescending silent commentary, "Well, of course, Manoah was only an Old Testament believer and didn't understand." On the contrary, Manoah understood perfectly and trembled. We must allow Manoah to be our teacher' (*Judges*, Christian Focus, 2000).

Respond

Ask God's Spirit to take hold of you. Rewrite verse 25, as if it were your story: 'The LORD's power began to strengthen [your name] … in [place where you live].'

Bible in a Year
1 Chronicles 19–21; Psalm 69

Tuesday
15 June

You be the judge

Prepare

'How is it, Lord, that I can fail, even when I'm close to you?'

Read Judges 14:1–20

Explore

A wedding story. What could be nicer? But again our expectations are confounded. This is not just a romance – it's Samson beginning to fulfill his predicted job description (13:5). But if you were looking for someone of unimpeachable integrity to measure out God's justice, you probably wouldn't pick Samson. Although, as a Nazirite, he was expected to live up to high standards – no touching corpses; no wine or beer; no trips to the barbers (see Numbers 6:1–5) – he soon manages to break one of these vows. The Spirit of the Lord may have taken hold of him, but as you read on, you can count for yourself the ways in which he fails to make the grade.

Having said that, he's brave, he's strong, and he's great fun. He's the life and soul of the party (Samson means 'sunny'). But the game goes horribly wrong and the wedding ends in disaster. His leonine anger precipitates the death of 30 Philistine men. Is this what God intended? Interestingly, the only times God's Spirit is mentioned in Judges 13–16 is when Samson attacks others or is attacked himself. So, if you're confused by God's choice, you're in good company (v 4). His ways are indeed beyond our understanding. But, as Paul points out, 'the mystery is that Christ lives in you' (Colossians 1:27, CEV).

Suddenly the power of the LORD made him strong, and he went down to Ashkelon, where he killed thirty men, stripped them, and gave their fine clothes to the men who had solved the riddle.

Judges 14:19a (GNB)

Respond

Meditate on
Psalm 51:3–7.

Bible in a Year
1 Chronicles 22,23; Galations 2

Payback time

Prepare

Are you easily offended? Think how you react when people make fun of you, your family, your country, your God.

Read   Judges 15:1–20

Explore

The wedding is over, but Samson has no wife. Everyone knows that she's been married off to his best man, but Samson is ignorant of this. And he is ignorant in a far more profound way – with little understanding of what it means to be dedicated to God. Like the rest of the Israelites, who have been called to live distinctively holy lives, Samson has been seduced by the Philistines. 'The two communities are so interlocked that even the Lord can find nothing to get hold of to prise them apart', suggests Michael Wilcock in *The Message of Judges* (The Bible Speaks Today series, IVP, 1992).

Freed from Egypt, God's people are again in a position where they are being ruled by the enemy – and content to be so, it seems (v 11). But now Samson's anger begins to drive a wedge between these two communities. For a moment, he appears as passive as his countrymen, but this is just the calm before the storm. The Spirit of the Lord is about to thunder through him, body and soul. For despite his faults, at least Samson knows who the enemy is and he is prepared to fight.

So 3,000 men of Judah went to the cave in the cliff at Etam and said to Samson, 'Don't you know that the Philistines are our rulers? What have you done to us?'

Judges 15:11 (GNB)

Respond

'Help me, Lord, when I get angry. Turn my rage around. Keep me aware of the enemy. Deliver me from committing evil.'

Bible in a Year
1 Chronicles 24–27; Galations 3

Bald truth

Prepare

'Lord, thank you for the strengths you have given me – from birth and since I've been following you.'

Read   Judges 16:1–22

Explore

If YouTube had been around in Samson's time, imagine how many people would have watched his gargantuan gate lift (v 3)! But, amazing as this feat was, it did not intimidate the Philistines – they knew their enemy and his weakness for women. Twenty years on, Samson hasn't changed. The only difference here is that instead of using a woman, a woman uses him. She, of course, is being used too, by the Philistine leaders.

If you were to ask the world's strongest man, Mariusz Pudzianowski, the secret of his strength, he would tell you it's malted milk! But Samson is more coy – and takes some time to admit to God's call on his life (v 17). In fact, he has become so self-sufficient he doesn't notice that the Spirit is missing (v 20b) and how blind he has become. He is literally blinded by the Philistines, but in many ways he appears to have been blind all along.

You may be feeling outraged by Samson's weaknesses, so ask yourself how well you'd do as a national leader. What would your strengths be? What would people see as your weaknesses? If the two were very separate, it would be easier to disentangle them. But, like Delilah's braid, our weaknesses are often woven in with our strengths.

> *She kept on asking him, day after day. He got so sick and tired of her nagging him about it that he finally told her the truth.*
>
> Judges 16:16,17a (GNB)

Respond

Whenever you fiddle with your hair today, remember you are a mixed bag of weaknesses and strengths. Ask God to untangle the two.

Bible in a Year
1 Chronicles 28,29; Psalms 70,71

Blind faith

Prepare

Who are the activists in our society? Are they characters you approve of, or do you feel uncomfortable about their methods? Pray for them.

Read   Judges 16:23–31

Explore

What starts as a fairytale ends as a tragedy – or is it a triumph? Samson's last act is one of faith and fulfils God's purpose (13:5) – a work which David will complete l00 years later – but at what cost? Samson's leadership seems morally ambiguous, leaving us with more questions than answers. What was admirable about Samson? Was his leadership brave or blind?

Perhaps it's easier to look at someone closer to us in time and then we might be able to appreciate the complexities of the situation. Dietrich Bonhoeffer was a prominent German theologian and a pacifist in the 1930s. Yet he could not stand on the sidelines and watch Hitler continue on his destructive path. Bonhoeffer's involvement in plans by members of the German Military Intelligence Office to assassinate Adolf Hitler resulted in his arrest in April 1943. 'The ultimate question for a responsible person to ask is not how he is to extricate himself heroically from the affair, but how the coming generation is to live,' he wrote to his fellow conspirators. He was later executed by hanging in April 1945, shortly before the end of the war. Was he a destroyer or a deliverer? Was his leadership brave or blind?

Respond

'Lord, help me to live responsibly and courageously. I could just stick my head in the sand. Instead, help me to look for solutions and to oppose what is wrong – to be brave, but not blind.'

Bible in a Year
2 Chronicles 1,2; Galations 4

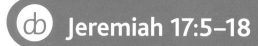
Saturday
19 June

Green leaves

Prepare

'Lord Jesus, your word has power. When you cursed the fig tree, it died. You deserve my respect.'

Read   Jeremiah 17:5–18

Explore

What was your country like in AD 1600? Think how it's changed and what has stayed the same. Are we any better than our ancestors? If you've been reading Samson's story this week, today's passage takes us forward 500 years. For a short while the kingdom of Israel was united under Saul, David and Solomon, but for much longer it was divided into two unequal halves: Israel and Judah. By 600 BC, each had a king, a capital city and a temple. But although, constitutionally, things had changed, the people's attitude towards God was the same as ever. They were no better than their ancestors. They had no sense of awe (v 15).

Jeremiah's task was to be a thorn in Judah's side, constantly challenging people to be loyal to God. As you read this conversation, listen out for his voice (vs 12–18) in response to the voice of the Lord (vs 5–11). Here is a man who was completely on God's side, championing his cause, like a tree drawing strength from God's fresh water stream (v 13). Here is a man whose name, clearly, has not disappeared in the dust. Do we need another Jeremiah today?

> LORD, heal me and I will be completely well; rescue me and I will be perfectly safe. You are the one I praise!
> Jeremiah 17:14 (GNB)

Respond

Water your plants today, and pray: 'Jesus, be the centre of my life. Keep me green and fruitful, even when the weather turns bad.'

Sunday
20 June

Tested
but rested

> But you, O LORD, are always my shield from danger; you give me victory and restore my courage.
>
> Psalm 3:3 (GNB)

Prepare

What's the weather like today, out of the window, and in your life?

Read   Psalm 3

Explore

The weather is definitely getting worse for David. As a charismatic leader, his job is to finish what Samson started and deliver the Israelites from the Philistines. But his own personal life impinges on his leadership and, in one of the most painful episodes of the Bible, he is forced to flee Jerusalem, weeping. Absalom, his son, has turned against him, seducing the loyalty of David's subjects. Together they plot to kill him in order to take his throne. Reading 2 Samuel 15–18 will help you to understand how David must be feeling at this moment.

Could you sleep well with all that going on around you? It would seem impossible. And yet David remains remarkably upbeat. Not only that, but as a compulsive writer he records what he feels. The American church leader Bill Hybels says, 'Character is who you are when no one's looking'. David's psalm show us what he was like when no one was looking – and what we find is an immense depth of trust in God. Imagine a world leader recording his times of crisis in a similar way today. Imagine them revealing what they're like when no one's looking. Imagine the Church reading their prayers and singing their songs. That's leadership of an altogether different kind!

Respond

'Make sure that your life sings the same song as your lips,' said the early church father Augustine. Seize the moment and make up your own short song as you start, or end, the day.

Bible in a Year
2 Chronicles 6,7; Galations 6

What would Jesus blog?

Feeling persecuted and abandoned, fearful about their future and surrounded on all sides by major pagan and occult influences, the seven churches featured in the first three chapters of Revelation were most definitely under pressure! Scattered over a wide 200-square mile area in Western Turkey, it seems that the relational link between them is the apostle John. Exiled by the authorities to the rocky island of Patmos, servant-prophet John received heavenly downloads for each of the seven Christ communities that he was connected with. Already paying a high price for his faith, he was about to become a significant messenger for Christ, delivering challenging words to a challenged church.

The believers in Ephesus, Smyrna, Pergamum, Thyatira, Sardis, Philadelphia and Laodicea could all top the league table of suffering Christians! They were struggling with the spread of emperor worship and the threat of the Roman authorities coming down hard upon them, they were tempted and compromised by the rise of paganism and occultism, and they were experiencing tensions with the Jews. Throw into the mix the usual trials of keeping your faith alive and making sure your passion for God stays burning bright, and you would have a fairly clear picture of their circumstances!

Jesus loves to communicate clearly, and each message follows a similar pattern. After the encouragement comes the bad news of their failings, finishing with a provocation to overcome and encouragement as to the eventual, ultimate reward. Very effective! Fascinating and informative, these messages are above all radically honest, relevant and alive with loving discipline.

Writer

Sue Rinaldi

Sue is a singer/songwriter and communicator. She travels internationally as a concert artist, worship coordinator, speaker and trainer. She is also a writer of books and articles and has been involved in TV and radio programmes.

Under pressure

Prepare

'Be still, and know that I am God' (Psalm 46:10). Take a few moments to do just that.

Read   Revelation 1:1–8

The revelation of Jesus Christ, which God gave him to show his servants what must soon take place. He made it known by sending his angel to his servant John …
Revelation 1:1 (NIV)

Explore

Poet-prophet John is about to embark upon a revealing of Jesus and of future events that will be mesmerising and shocking! At the beginning of this enthralling exposé, we find that John has been chosen by Almighty God to deliver first century 'blogs' to seven churches under pressure (vs 1,2).

Times were turbulent for these early believers. Surrounded by major pagan and occult influences, under threat of persecution by the Roman authorities, and wrestling with issues of determining faith from heresy, these significant communities were about to receive a download that would challenge them to the core (v 4)! Wisely, John establishes the credentials of the divine author with astounding clarity. Already submerged within an eye-catching image of a triumphant Jesus, he applauds the Lord for being the absolute, the A–Z, the ancient-present-future One (v 8).

How amazing and humbling to be called a *servant* of God? When so many other voices vie for our allegiance, it takes dedication and passion to live a life of worshipful surrender to the Lord. John has these qualities and unashamedly boasts of the timeless traits of the Sovereign-Strong. Is it any wonder that God speaks to such a heart?

Respond

When people speak your name, would they call you a servant of God? Think through the day ahead and imagine what this service to God might look like.

Bible in a Year
2 Chronicles 8,9; Psalm 72

Tuesday
22 June

Lost in wonder

Prepare

We are commanded to worship God. Answer this call to worship by offering up words of thankfulness and praise.

Read

Revelation 1:9–20

Explore

Many DVD movies come packed with bonus features, and the most illuminating are usually the interviews with the writers and producers. We learn how the story began and we get to appreciate some of the circumstances that helped them interpret and finally deliver the plot to a wide audience.

Similarly, here we are treated to some of the behind-the-scenes data on John, and the overwhelming impression is that he is a worshipper (v 10)! Exiled on Patmos for preaching the gospel, he was presumably deep in worship and prayer on the Lord's Day when the vision and voice of Christ broke through.

Aware of the clouds of persecution gathering and already paying a high price for his witness to Jesus, it is from a place of worship that the apocalyptic adventure unfolds. As John hears a trumpet-clear voice, as his eyes count seven lamp stands and seven stars, and as he absorbs the fire-blaze brilliance of Christ, he immediately recognises a deeply significant sacred encounter (v 16).

Precious and challenging words were about to be spoken to John – a heavenly delivery straight to the heart of a worshipper (v 19).

> *I am the Living One; I was dead, and behold I am alive for ever and ever! And I hold the keys of death and Hades.*
> Revelation 1:18 (NIV)

Respond

There are many reasons why our ears become dull to the voice of God. When God speaks, what is your response? Do you respond with awe? Or have you become so familiar with your Creator that you have lost the wonder?

Bible in a Year
2 Chronicles 10–12; Ephesians 1

Wednesday
23 June

All you need
is love

Yet I hold this against you: You have forsaken your first love.
Revelation 2:4 (NIV)

Prepare

Recall the names of those you love, and pray for God's strength and help today in their lives.

Read Revelation 2:1–12

Explore

The good, the bad, and the challenging! That seems to be the pattern for the messages to the seven churches in western Turkey. First up is cosmopolitan Ephesus – a thriving gateway to Asia. Host to the annual games, it was also academically and financially strong, and infamous for its thousands of priests and priestesses, many of whom were sacred prostitutes. Jesus encourages the church by recognising its perseverance and courage, and its refusal to tolerate immorality and religious pretenders (v 2). Extreme praise considering they were living within a culture described by theologian William Barclay as the 'Vanity Fair of the Ancient World'. Ethically and theologically they were in good shape, but they had lost one vital thing – love for God and one another (v 4). Their passion had been replaced by doctrinal obedience and duty.

There is no mistaking the priority Jesus places on love, and this challenge resonates today (v 5). Living within a toxic society poisoned by corruption and selfish ambition, we are also called back to love. Ephesus thought they had everything, but in reality had nothing of any eternal value. Conversely, the church in Smyrna were plagued by their poverty and yet were described as 'rich'. The difference? Love!

Respond

Has love taken a back seat in your life? Have other motives and driving forces taken over? Be aware of the power of love as you meet people today.

Bible in a Year
2 Chronicles 13–15; Ephesians 2

Thursday
24 June

And the winner is…!

Prepare

'Your word is a lamp to my feet and a light for my path' (Psalm 119:105).

Read

Revelation 2:12–17

Explore

Every year there is an award for the 'Worst UK High Street'. Recently the title was given to a town not far from me and the stigma of being awarded this dubious accolade kick-started some serious regeneration! If being known for having the most run-down, visitor unfriendly and economically depressed high street is bad, imagine being branded as 'where Satan has his throne' (v 13)! The academic city of Pergamum was the recipient of this dark title. Perhaps this was due to the dominating Altar of Zeus where smoke from countless sacrifices would constantly rise, or because of the proliferation of idol worship (v 14). Or maybe it was the presence of the Christian-persecuting Roman proconsul, and the ungodly emphasis placed upon emperor worship.

The Pergamum believers were constantly being enticed into abandoning and renouncing their faith, and Jesus issues a clear warning to stay loyal and true (v 13). It is alarming how popular but erroneous doctrine or distorted spirituality can dumb down or twist our understanding of the Christian faith. How difficult to swim against the tide when the waves are carrying us away from our God-source. Yet Christ calls us to overcome… and for every one who does, there is an award (v 17)!

> *To him who overcomes, I will give some of the hidden manna. I will also give him a white stone with a new name written on it, known only to him who receives it.*
> **Revelation 2:17b (NIV)**

Respond

Are there situations when you feel like you're swimming against the tide? Is it sometimes hard to walk the holy way? Remember that God is your guide and your strength.

Bible in a Year
2 Chronicles 16,17; Psalm 73

Just say no!

I know your deeds, your love and faith, your service and perseverance, and that you are now doing more than you did at first.

Revelation 2:19 (NIV)

Prepare

'Where can I go from your Spirit? Where can I flee from your presence?' (Psalm 139:7). Focus on the wonder of these words.

Read

Revelation 2:18–29

Explore

Computers get it. Hospital wards are renowned for it. Global pandemics can be caused by it. Apparently, even churches can be afflicted by it. A virus! They are dangerous and they spread.

A close neighbour to Pergamum, the church of Thyatira was under threat from a strain of teaching that was bringing confusion and compromise. To do business in this market city, everyone was required to join a trade guild. These guilds, however, were more than industrial unions. They were deeply involved in sexual immorality and idolatry (v 20). A conundrum indeed! By opting out you essentially ruin all possibilities for trading. By opting in you are seen to be participating in Christ-denying behaviour, regardless of the fact you are earning an income for your family. Which is a good thing… right?

Wrong! Jesus demands clear and direct obedience and challenges the believers to just say no. Compromise will mean abandoning certain values and trading them for others. The amazing thing is that by saying no there is a reward (v 26). Experience shows that you play with fire until the fire starts playing with you. So to avoid getting burnt, our ears must be tuned to the Spirit of God (v 29).

Respond

Are you playing with fire? Are there any compromises you are making? Today, if you hear God speaking, do not reject the call to follow Christ.

Bible in a Year
2 Chronicles 18–20; Ephesians 3

Saturday
26 June

Surprise, surprise!

Prepare

Consider the example of Jesus when he washed the disciples' feet. What do you learn from this?

Read
Matthew 24:36–51

Explore

Some people are mystery shoppers. They turn up at a restaurant, cinema or business undetected, unknown and unannounced, and observe whether it is performing to the highest of standards. A comprehensive report indicates areas of effectiveness as well as areas in need of improvement. The whole idea is to see people's true colours – how they really are and what values they really care about. In a similar way the return visit of Jesus is unknown, except by the Father (v 36). We are therefore encouraged to keep watch and maintain godly standards of behaviour and not become lazy or shameful (v 42). The supreme quality our Maker and Master is looking for is faithfulness (v 45).

In order to make this point, Matthew uses the analogy of servants who have been put in charge of their master's household. The servant who abuses that trust and ignores his responsibilities will be punished (v 51). But the true servant is the one who carries out his master's wishes with wisdom and consistency, not getting sidetracked by other things. We may have started our walk of faith with godly intentions and a spirit-filled passion, but have we become distracted? Perhaps it's time to consider again the wishes of our Master and follow them.

> *Therefore keep watch, because you do not know on what day your Lord will come.*
>
> Matthew 24:42 (NIV)

Respond

If there are any ways in which you know you have been unfaithful to Christ, then ask for forgiveness and God-strength to live differently.

Bible in a Year
2 Chronicles 21–23; Ephesians 4

107

Sunday
27 June

Broken promises!

> *Come, let us sing for joy to the LORD; let us shout aloud to the Rock of our salvation.*
> Psalm 95:1 (NIV)

Prepare

Is there a song that expresses your thanks to God right now? Either listen to it, or if you can, sing it.

Read   Psalm 95

Explore

My time as a Brownie was very short-lived! The initial promise to 'do my best, to love my God, to serve the Queen and my country, to help other people and to keep the Brownie Guide Law' was spoken with an initial burst of enthusiasm, but soon broken and ignored. I was never a fan of the uniform but even less enamoured with the idea of having to think of others and do a good deed every day. Soon, I had forgotten my promise and hardened my heart towards the whole idea!

In a multiplicity of ways, that slide into rebellion is world-wearingly familiar. A marriage, a relationship, a team or a project can all suffer from disinterest and disruption, and before you know it, a once-favoured partnership is dangerously on the rocks. The psalm is calling people back to the Lord. Even the Israelites, who had witnessed first hand the miracles of God, had hardened their hearts towards him and strayed (v 10). Hard to believe? Probably not, because we know the shape of our own hearts.

That is why these verses are reminding us of the greatness of God, the highest King, the mountain maker, the wonderful creator who loves us and longs for us to follow him (vs 1–7). Words to melt the hardest of hearts!

Respond

Are you in need of a little softening? Has your heart hardened to the love of God? It's time to tender up!

Bible in a Year
2 Chronicles 24,25; Ephesians 5

After the gold rush

Prepare

What attributes or aspects of God mean the most to you right now?

Read
Revelation 3:1–6

Explore

The film *Music and Lyrics* features an eighties pop star basking in his former glory. With equal amounts of amusement and embarrassment, the central character finally comes to life again after resurrecting his writing talent and finding fresh success. Sardis was a city with a reputation for greatness, and also basking in a previous glory. Unfortunately, this former gold rush city was most definitely not glittering anymore. Instead it was asleep and, apparently, so was the church. In fact, it was so asleep it was about to die (v 2)!

I have heard people say, 'good is the enemy of great'. I imagine we can all cite examples of feeling intoxicated by a good reputation or from receiving praise for certain achievements. But then enthusiasm for progress wanes and complacency, ineffectiveness and pride soon gather round. Jesus sounds the alarm and summons the church in Sardis to wake up from the sleeping sickness that has infected the body. Even their deeds have become futile! It is now time for genuine remorse and to actively walk into the future with Christ (vs 3,4). That is indeed a challenge to our frantic and fast-paced lives. Busy does not automatically mean fruitful. And past success does not guarantee future victory.

Remember, therefore, what you have received and heard; obey it, and repent. But if you do not wake up, I will come like a thief, and you will not know at what time I will come to you.

Revelation 3:3 (NIV)

Respond

Is Jesus asking you to 'wake up'? Have you become apathetic and ineffective in any area of your life and faith?

Bible in a Year
2 Chronicles 26–28; Psalm 74

Tuesday
29 June

Against
all odds

> Since you have kept my command to endure patiently, I will also keep you from the hour of trial that is going to come upon the whole world to test those who live on the earth.
>
> Revelation 3:10 (NIV)

Prepare

Take a fresh look at the cross and the extreme love that Jesus demonstrated. What is your response?

Read — Revelation 3:7–13

Explore

I love stories that chart the struggle of the underdog. It's so inspiring to see the apparently insignificant conquer the supposedly superior competition. The tenacity and perseverance required for such contests is enormous. The church in Philadelphia demonstrated those prized qualities. They even receive high praise from Christ himself (v 8).

Philadelphia was a relatively new city, famous for its vineyards and volcano. But in amongst the wine and the danger, it was the Jews that were causing the greatest tremors. The significant Jewish communities were hostile to the Christians, not least because they considered the worship of a crucified criminal as Messiah to be blasphemous! John delivers strong words as he forecasts the fate of their accusers (v 9).

Where is God when it hurts? Nancy Guthrie, an American mother whose second daughter was diagnosed with the same disorder as her recently deceased first daughter, said her 'suffering was a harrowing invitation to a higher dialogue', and in the darkest of days she 'experienced supernatural strength and peace'. The believers in Philadelphia accepted the invitation for a higher dialogue and, in return for their patient endurance, God promises an open door of opportunity (v 8).

Respond

'Consider it pure joy … whenever you face trials of many kinds, because you know that the testing of your faith develops perseverance' (James 1:2–4). Does this passage describe you? When did you last get tested and experience joy?

Bible in a Year
2 Chronicles 29,30; Ephesians 6

Red hot
and holy!

Prepare

Do you feel fully involved within a community of believers? How important is that to you?

Read

Revelation 3:14–22

Explore

There is an excellent reason why coffee shops feature hot drinks alongside delicious iced specialities – because lukewarm just does not hit the spot! And that is the precise complaint Jesus has regarding the church in Laodicea (v 16). The city faced challenges concerning its water supply and so the metaphor John uses speaks perfectly into their situation. They knew the insipidness and ineffectiveness of lukewarm water – it was good for nothing!

There was a self sufficiency about the wealthy Laodicea – a smugness that arose from their ability to rebuild the city after an earthquake had brought major devastation. They were pleased with their achievements and proud of their independence, but Jesus delivers a sting that speaks right into this (vs 17,18). We are designed to live in community and not in isolation. It is dangerous to believe that we can exist without others. Independence from God and from others is not the mark of a God-centred church. In amongst these strong words, Jesus communicates something of extreme importance. Love and discipline work together! It is only because Jesus loves them, that he delivers such a weighty provocation. Healthy discipline is an invitation to learn. It is essentially a matter of love (vs 19,20).

> *Here I am! I stand at the door and knock. If anyone hears my voice and opens the door, I will come in and eat with him, and he with me.*
> **Revelation 3:20 (NIV)**

Respond

The inescapable truth is that Christ disciplines those he loves. How do you respond when disciplined? Do you see it as a means for growth or as a direct threat to your freedom?

Bible in a Year
2 Chronicles 31,32; Luke 1:1–38

Fast food has never been so healthy!

Head down to Rocky's Plaice, the best fish and chip shop in town, to discover more about knowing Jesus and the difference it can make to you!

A complete holiday club based on stories of Peter from Acts.

Bible engagement, games, drama, craft, chat, songs and more!

£9.99

£19.99

£10.00

includes photocopiable resources PLUS free extras online

A Scripture Union holiday club programme
great **new ideas** inspired by experience

Rocky's Plaice DVD features: five storytelling episodes, a training feature, songs, pdfs of artwork, music and lots more.

Rocky's Menu contains the essential Bible text, activities and extra information, together with pages to enable children to personalise the books.

Buy locally at your Christian Bookstore
Buy online www.scriptureunion.org.uk/featured
Buy direct 0845 07 06 006 quoting DB
or see order form